ReVISION *of* GOD

Also by Beverley Tasker

ReVISION
of
GOD

---

*the thinking person's
introduction
to d-i-y religion*

H. BEVERLEY TASKER

Loebertas

First published in 2003 by
Loebertas
7 Church Lane, Long Ashton, North Somerset, BS41 9LU

ISBN 1 874316 49 X

Designed and typeset by Loebertas
Printed and bound in Great Britain by J W Arrowsmith Ltd

*...disturbing the universe
of our accepted assumptions...*

PREFACE

What I have to say in this little book doesn't come easily. I recognise that in its critical analysis of institutional religion and the images of God that prevail today it may ruffle a few feathers. But I believe it will also serve to liberate people from beliefs that have become tired and unworkable.

My aim has been to develop an understanding of God, the universe and our own lives which reconciles the truths of religion and science and at the same time helps to bind humanity together in peace. If this aim is achieved even in some small way the effort will have been worth it.

HBT
July 2003

ACKNOWLEDGEMENTS

—Quotations from *The Holy Bible* are from The Authorized Version unless otherwise stated.

—Extracts from the Authorized Version of the Bible (The King James Bible), the rights in which are vested in the Crown, are reproduced by permission of the Crown's Patentee, Cambridge University Press.

—The New English Bible (NEB) © Oxford University Press and Cambridge University Press 1961, 1970.

—Extracts from The Holy Bible Revised Standard Version (RSV) are reproduced courtesy of HarperCollins.

—Extract from The Book of Common Prayer, the rights in which are vested in the Crown, are reproduced by permission of the Crown's Patentee, Cambridge University Press.

All other acknowledgements are included under the appropriate Bibliographical Reference at the end of this book.

CONTENTS

Prologue

Moment of Truth

Midway through the course of this life.

Dante, *Inferno*

It was a late Sunday afternoon in Autumn. The echoes of Evensong were fading from our beautiful country church. As parishioners bade each other farewell and wended their way homeward in the twilight I knew something was not quite right. Wondering what it was I locked the door of the church and slowly walked under the lime trees along the path back to the Rectory. Once inside, I stood at the study window looking out towards the fields. It was almost dark.

Then it happened. I found myself speaking to my own reflection. "You don't believe a word of what you have just preached!"

An exquisite moment of crisis had arrived. For years I had given sermons that contained what I considered to be faithful representations of Christian belief. But during Evensong a few minutes earlier it had all finally dried up. Why? Because in that moment I realised I had simply been reproducing words that thousands of vicars had spoken over many years and those words no longer belonged to me. They were second hand. As I stared round the room at all my books and notes it slowly occurred to me that either it was all in vain or there had to be another way.

I acted fairly swiftly after that, ringing up the bookseller in town next day and getting him to do a valuation of all those volumes which I had spent years collecting. He came along, cheerfully surveyed the books, offered me a good price and bought the lot except for Peake's Commentary, a gift from my wife, and a Greek New Testament, given by the Bishop at my ordination, both of which I decided to keep. Everything else went. The bookshelves were left quite bare. Parishioners who came into the study afterwards thought I'd had a breakdown. Perhaps they were right! But something *had* broken down. And something had to change. It did.

When a problem arises the only solution is to go back to the roots and sort it out from there. So if the Faith was rooted in Scripture that was where my problem lay. And that was where it had to be solved. What followed changed my view of things entirely, causing a considerable amount of intellectual searching, setting me at odds with much that passes for sound belief, separating me at times from the mainstream Church, but bringing an undeniable sense of peace.

I knew some Greek and a little Hebrew so I invested in grammar books and lexicons to find out for myself what those Scriptures actually said rather than having to accept what English translators had passed down to us. And here I was in for another shock. In passage after passage, word after word, the original often bore no resemblance to its translations, and was certainly capable of a different interpretation from the ones on offer.

I could see why the Church was failing. The true Word was simply not being proclaimed at all. In spite of preaching from texts translated into some of the finest literature in the English language, we were nevertheless thinking of truth in a sense quite different from what was intended.

This led to a further conclusion. I could have been wildly wrong but it did seem very clear not only that Christianity had become heavily institutionalised but that the Scriptures themselves had been translated by the Church for the specific purpose of perpetuating the institution. And possibly this was why generations had deserted the Church over the recent decades of our history. We were speaking to the people but they were not listening any more, and that was because we were speaking to them on behalf of the institution. It was now time to speak to the institution on behalf of the people. It has taken me years to be able to state this with confidence. The Church was now getting in the way of the message it had been set up to proclaim. The crisis I had experienced that late afternoon was not my crisis alone. It was the crisis of the Church itself.

Part One

A Church by Law Established

Chapter 1

The Numbers Game

We are just statistics, born to consume resources.

Horace, *Epistles*

The Western Church seems to be fond of gathering together statistics, and the newspapers are equally attached to reporting them. But this fascination with figures and trends has not served the Church well in recent times, especially in Europe and particularly in England.

For instance, at the time of the great census of 1851 there were seventeen million people in England and Wales. Out of these eight million went to Church, four million to the Church of England. One quarter of the population attended the Church of England. Even these statistics caused some alarm at the time. *Only* a quarter! A century and a half later there are sixty million people in the United Kingdom. Of these less than one million attend the Church of England, just *one sixtieth*. That in any factual reckoning amounts to a staggering decline.

There are caveats. Until quite recently it was a familiar and well-rehearsed argument in England and on the Continent that although people didn't go to church regularly they at least attended for baptisms, weddings and funerals. Youngsters were confirmed into membership of the Church and went to the church youth club. These facts helped the statistics. But there has been dramatic change here too. For example, since UK legislation in the 1990s a whole new world has opened up for those tying the knot. You can now marry in a hotel, under the sea, whilst flying on top of an aircraft or as you cling to a rock face. If you like the touch of religion you can always find a clergyman somewhere to oblige. There are humanist funerals, and ceremonies at register offices to replace christenings in churches. In some quarters confirmations have virtually disappeared. With the choice now available the statistics of the Church present a fairly sorry picture.

Almost forty years ago, the then Bishop of Woolwich painted this portrait of the future of the Church:

> What, then, is the prospect for the Church? Outwardly it is an enigma, inwardly a mystery. All one can be sure of is that it is bound to be morning *and* night, darkness *and* dawn.
>
> Speaking simply from within the situation one knows in England, I become increasingly convinced that the flags of dawn are likely to appear only out of a night a good deal darker yet. For it is not only academic theology which has been living on its own fat. The supply of fat is running out also for the Church...The fat, represented still, for instance, by the inflated figures for infant baptism, could easily be cut by fifty per cent in a generation.
>
> John Robinson, *The New Reformation?*

Here John Robinson was addressing the situation in the Church of England, as one of its bishops, although he included other denominations in his survey and analysis. What was true then, and is true now, of the Church of England is no less true of the wider Episcopal Church, even in the United States of America where churchgoing is considered to be strong.

Statistics, of course, are only part of the scene. The Church in many areas does flourish. But the facts are there in front of us and have been for some time.

Chapter 2

Heads in the Sand

We are deceived by the appearance of right.

Horace, *De arte poetica*

Facts of decline are always greeted by leaders as though nothing has happened. In the eighteenth century, when threats were made to the Church's established position, the Church and State rallied together and proclaimed that all was well. Tobias Smollett describes a debate in the House of Lords in 1705 with a resolution which ends:

> whoever goes about to suggest or insinuate that the church is in danger, under her Majesty's administration, is an enemy to the Queen, the church, and the Kingdom.

Tobias Smollett, *The History of England*

This rather compliant attitude was not shared by everyone, however. Jonathan Swift, the eighteenth-century Dean, satirist and poet, wrote to a friend:

> I have long given up all hope of Church or Christianity.

Jonathan Swift, cited in
C H Sisson, *Is There a Church of England?*

Sisson records that Swift had heard of an author who was of the opinion that 'the Christian Religion will not last above 300 and odd years'. Whoever that author was his prescient remarks cannot be ignored for much longer. If people have been predicting for over three hundred years that the National Religion would decline to the point of extinction, and if little has changed within the Church to arrest that decline, then perhaps we should let nature take its course. As Shelley said, where eyes are shut nothing can be seen. But Sisson would not allow for this expedient of fate.

> Swift is to be taken seriously. The decline he foresaw has gone on, of late very rapidly, to the point at which the inhabitants of this kingdom show not so much an aversion from the Church as a disregard for it, as an institution, while claims to be more Christian than the Church, or merely more honest, are heard on all sides.

C H Sisson, *Is There a Church of England?*

Here we have it. In the past there has been a natural sense of identification between Church and Christianity. It now seems that this symmetry is being broken. It is often said that you don't have to go to Church to be a Christian. It is also only too apparent that you don't have to be a Christian to go to Church. Perhaps that is how it should be—the Church should be there for all. But more and more the Church of England has taken on the characteristics of a sect. And in so doing it has unwittingly all but severed its links with other churches, the State and, worst of all, with Christianity itself.

25

Chapter 3

Are you Downbeat or Upbeat?

*"There are many roads to God, Robert, but
I have always considered the Church of England
to be the M1, so to speak."*

Dick Clement & Ian La Frenais, *Whatever
Happened to the Likely Lads?*

Only recently have people begun to wake up to the fact that something very serious is happening to Christianity in the United Kingdom. Towards the end of 2001 Dr David Voas, a demographer at the University of Sheffield, quoted figures that substantiate the prophecy by Bishop Robinson almost four decades earlier.

> By doing a careful year-by-year calculation of births, christenings, mortality, migration, and so on, I was recently able to arrive at a good estimate of the notionally Anglican (as defined by christening) population. In 2001 this group dropped below 50 per cent of the total number of British subjects living in England.
>
> David Voas, 'Is Britain a Christian country?'

Dr Voas' findings should send shock signals throughout the Church of England:

> For the first time since the Church was founded,
> then, nominal adherents of the established faith
> are in a minority. England is no longer an
> Anglican country.
>
> ibid.

As if this isn't bad enough he calculates the trend of
baptisms within the Anglican church over the next few
years:

> The Church is losing a million christened
> Anglicans every five years as the baptized die
> without being replaced. Losses will continue at
> that level for at least three decades, unless there is
> a dramatic resurgence in the popularity of
> christening. By the end of the century the
> notionally Anglican community will be less than
> half the size that it is today, even assuming there
> are no further declines in baptism rates.
>
> ibid.

These predictions may of course be ignored, but they
are still there for all to see.

No doubt the influx of different religions into Europe
in recent years and the rapid and deliberate
secularisation of our social patterns of life have
contributed heavily to the sharp decline in the number
of worshipping Christians in England. But whatever the
cause, the effects are severe. According to Dr Voas:

> To judge purely by church attendance Britain is
> not very Christian, nor is Christian England very
> Anglican. The best estimate for Sunday church
> attendance in Great Britain in 2000 was just
> below eight per cent of the population...Only
> about a quarter of those attending in England are

27

worshipping in the Church of England; they are
substantially outnumbered by Catholics at mass.

ibid.

The multi-cultural, multi-religious society is at
present working to the disadvantage of the Church. But
this is because the Church is weak and vacillating in its
approach to the cultural, spiritual and intellectual life in
this country and throughout the Western world. How
did this state of affairs arise? Why is the Church so
weak and heavy laden? Why is it losing members at
such a fast rate? And is its decline really attributable to
the presence of other religions or are all religions in
their different ways faced with the same prospects?

The Church of England's response to statistics has
always been consistent. With its skilful deployment of
the English language towards the avoidance of truth, it
employs three words: *challenge, opportunity,* and
exciting. How often do we hear Church officials issue
statements such as *this presents the Church with
a challenge* or *the Church is faced with many
opportunities*? Many of us have been aware of the
overall challenge facing the Church for some
considerable time. There are greater challenges with
each statistical report. We should like to know how the
Church proposes to deal with these challenges. What is
the underlying cause? The repetition of a few stock
phrases is no longer sufficient. Nor are diversionary
lectures on market forces or politics, or the Church's
simplistic pronouncements on social divisions in the
country at large. The Church of England may be
challenged by its own opportunities, but we are not
excited any more. There are other things to think about,
real challenges to meet: the removal of grinding

28

poverty, for instance, or meeting intellectual doubt with convincing argument.

> So long as one believes in God one has the right *to do* the Good in order *to be* moral...And since it is a question of being moral in God's eyes, in order to praise him, to aid him in his creation, the subordination of doing to being is legitimate...It is legitimate to be the most beautiful of all, the best possible. The egoism of the saint is sanctioned. But when God dies and the saint is no more than an egoist, then what difference does it make that he has a beautiful soul, that he is beautiful, if only to himself?

> Jean-Paul Sartre, *Notebooks for an Ethics*

This is how many people think at present and helps to explain perhaps why some feel that belief in God has a tinge of hypocrisy about it. Recently a bereaved parent mentioned someone she knew who had also been through a difficult time. That person had experienced loss, tragedy and inexplicable misfortune, all in a relatively short period. She couldn't take any more and "had given up on God"—after all, what is the point when you end up suffering like this? she said. It is a question frequently asked. We run out of words when we hear such stories. To say that this provides the Church with an opportunity, or that we must be seen to care, sounds cheap in the presence of doubt that has grown out of bitter personal experience.

> I am weary of my crying...while I wait for my God.

> *The Holy Bible,* Psalm 69: 3

The Psalmist, Sartre, Beckett and similar writers show just as much compassion in framing questions about a world without God as does the enthusiast for God who seeks to convert everybody to the Faith and uses suffering or fear as a tool to do so. Gradually as people experience such a world, and witness the incapacity of the Church to deal with it, individual doubt is absorbed into the general culture.

There are many reasons behind the decline of the Church. One, though, has to be faced sooner rather than later. The Church's image of God is no longer sustainable. It so often takes the existence of God for granted without caring to define what it means by 'God' and ignores the fact that for a considerable number of people today belief in the God of the Church doesn't work. They see God portrayed through the eyes of an institution and they have rejected the portrait. And for us to go on repeating the message that has been rejected is a bit like someone giving answers to questions people are not asking any more. It reveals the inflexibility of a static institution.

Could it be, therefore, that the Church has become a *substitute* for the Christian Faith? The Church itself, naturally, would reject such an idea. But it is worth examining the case to see if the institution of the Church stands up to scrutiny and whether or not it can justify its existence for much longer. Such an examination will inevitably cause a good deal of pain. I hesitate to launch into it for the very reason that this could be interpreted as a kind of disloyalty, a negative approach when we all need to look on the bright side. What I have to offer here, however, is not a cynical view of something which some, including myself, find precious and worthy. The question is this: when people look at the Church do they see a Church engaged with its own affairs or are they inspired to look beyond?

Chapter 4

The Cost of Stewardship

He cannot flatter, he,
An honest mind and plain, he must speak truth:
An they will take it, so.

William Shakespeare, *King Lear*, II.ii.104

Many will agree that the separation of the institutional Church as a whole from the Christianity it represents is due in no small measure to the structures of the Church itself. The Church, for those people, has actually become an obstacle to Faith. As with most institutions, the edifice of self preservation has simply got in the way. For the Church to be in this position as the representative of one of the most ascetic and unworldly religions is understandable perhaps because of its political constitution, but it is unacceptable in every other sense. Let us see why—even though our brief analysis may involve us in a few tedious points of domestic insularity.

The first thing to acknowledge is that not only are the structures of the Church proving cumbersome and awkward but they require ever increasing financial support. If this were not the case the Church would not need to spend so much time talking about money. The

Church seems to give the impression to the outsider, and often to those on the inside, that it simply preaches the gospel of its own salvation. However skilfully this is disguised it is detectable. You go to church on holiday and the notices are about fund-raising. You attend a meeting of the clergy with their bishop or archdeacon and the topic under discussion? Money. Parishes have joined together, yet costs continue to rise. We are told there is no problem yet everywhere there is a shortage of cash. One almost feels sorry for the Church. But not quite.

The Church is trying to face in two directions at once. It is making every effort to bolster the morale of the clergy and parishioners by pretending all is well while at the same time putting more and more burden on the shoulders of fewer people. And this is no longer to further the Christian cause. The Church is now being tempted to use the Christian Faith and the Scriptures themselves to support arguments for its own survival. There are examples of this everywhere. But it simply will not do to try to prop up an institution as great as the Church of England has been in the past in this haphazard and slightly dishonest way.

Much of the Church's troubles are self-inflicted, and the sympathy of the nation, and of church people, is running out. It is clearly the case that demands on parishes are rapidly exceeding the ability to meet them. Crisis is undoubtedly looming. As costs continue to rise and numbers fall it is only a matter of time before the Church of England collapses under its own weight.

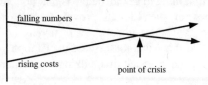

It is regrettable that in the absence of a firm policy with radical and long lasting solutions the institution of the Church simply asks for more money to keep the status quo. A question seldom put is why do we need *more* money to fund an organisation that has fewer working clergy and holds less appeal for the population as the years roll by? The point to make here is that—as with our National Health Service, for example—to pour more money into the institution could well exacerbate the very conditions that make more money necessary. So the situation never improves. In fact it may be the *wrong* thing to do to reinforce a system that stands in need of fundamental change, because it will never see the need for such change so long as it is kept going by artificial means.

The Church is not going to succeed with this kind of attitude. The ineffectual moderateness of Anglicanism is leading towards a vacuum. Like the grin of the Cheshire Cat in *Alice in Wonderland*, the benign smile of the Church will no doubt stretch beyond the point of collapse. But it will simply be met by polite sadness as the people turn away and get on with life. Much the way it is now, in fact.

Chapter 5

Led by the Lord?

This above all: to thine own self be true.

William Shakespeare, *Hamlet*, I.iii.78

The Church today inherits a form of ministry that extends back to the days of the Scriptures. Indeed the Scriptures are considered to be its axiomatic basis. It would depart from this foundation at its peril. But what is this basis? And can it throw light on other religions?

In the New Testament Christ chose apostles. They lived simply and frugally but had a serious and dangerous job to do: to proclaim the Kingdom of God, the Good News. The way the Church has handled this over the years, though, has tended so to dilute the meaning of 'Good News' that these words are now an embarrassment to the population at large. They make us feel uncomfortable and unable to dissociate them from smirking cranks with slippery intentions.

At great moments in its history the Church has been recognised by all sections of society for its profundity of thought, its beautiful and sustaining liturgies and the deepest respect for the Divine Godhead. It spearheaded work in education, setting up trusts and foundations for the poor, many of them now Oxbridge colleges for example. It led the way in treating and caring for the sick and the elderly by founding hospitals and almshouses, the remaining ones still named after saints. It created monasteries and cathedrals of such awe-inspiring splendour that people have marvelled at their architecture and magnificent art ever since. The Church didn't seek 'to be relevant' or try to convince the world that it had 'a role in the modern age', but saw what needed to be done and did it, with devotion to service, a pursuit of excellence and a boundless compassion for those who were less fortunate in society.

Throughout the ages this vision has occasionally been lost. Some periods in the Church's history have given cause for shame and regret. The Gospel at times has been reduced to a slick formula for worldly success, as we see in the luxuriant corruption of the Church of the Popes towards the close of the Medieval period, or it has become the pretext for violent crime against humanity, especially in the Crusades and later in the Religious Wars of the sixteenth century. But the Church has survived until now in spite of these ambivalent relations between power and service.

Today, however, we are at the cross roads. We have reached a crisis point similar to those seemingly far off days but in the opposite sense. In the past the Church has been too strong. Now it isn't strong enough. One has to be very careful here, but it is now widely recognised that the Gospel is frequently weakened by those who proclaim it. Individuals who look to the Church for guidance in their lives often find themselves at the hands of an evangelical organisation that behaves like a recruiting agency for Jesus. Yet many of those Christians who wave the Bible about and sound

35

judgement upon others are not always the ones who convince us by their own character. There seems to be a certain type of person who claims to be 'led by the Lord', who assumes authority but carries no weight. Such people often have the supercilious grin of those who think they know the truth but stand a million miles away from it. They believe that God is always in personal attendance to their every whim, that he answers prayer in such a way as to provide for their daily needs: the right holiday, or car, or insurance policy; that God is in fact a fixer of broken deals. In the way they speak God seems little more than a chap 'up there', with a benevolent smile and plenty of handouts for all those who love him and a frown and a set of rotten circumstances for those who disobey his rules.

Tolerance is a virtue not found in great abundance amongst such people. Their foundation is a narrow literalism, which excludes more than it includes. That is why they cling together in clusters of fellowships, afraid to admit anyone who is not 'of the Lord'. Breadth and depth are not terms usually associated with their thought patterns, which appear simplistic and formula-driven. They are the new fundamentalists and they are rising in number and confidence. Their trust in the Lord is possibly a psychological prop, satisfying temporarily their own inadequacies, but the damage they are doing to the Christian Faith is incalculable.

Chapter 6

Literalist or Illiterate?

I moralize two meanings in one word.

William Shakespeare, *Richard III*, III.i.83

Fundamentalist Christians and literal interpreters of the Bible insist that every word in the Bible is true. What exactly this means is open to question. Does it mean that every *English* word in the Bible is true? If so how do we reconcile this view with the many known mistranslations down the years (18,000 in the Authorised Version alone), or the numerous variant texts and, not least, the personal element of interpretation in translation? Or do we infer that it is the original texts that are word for word true? If we do, then—which text? The constructed texts of the New Testament? The codex Sinaiticus, or the Vaticanus? The Masoretic Hebrew text in the Hermitage—is that true? The Masoretic text is less than a thousand years old. And do we take our English version from that or other contemporary texts, or from the pre-Christian Septuagint translation into Greek that precedes all Hebrew versions?

The statement 'every word in the Bible is true' is itself untrue, and very misleading. The simplistic view is that the text was all there present and correct at the beginning and all we did was translate it into English. This attitude has caused the Church to lose its grip on the teaching aspect of Christianity, and has led to a breakdown of doctrine. It has also brought into the Church itself, or at least to the perimeters of Christian belief, a rigid frame of mind that cannot readily and warmly adjust to varied human enquiry. Bigotry is not far removed from the humourless and patronising view expressed by so many literalist interpreters of the Bible. The fundamentalist position requires radical revision if it is to be respected and given any valid position within the Christian Church.

Chapter 7

The Liberal West

What is new is always fine.

French proverb

In addition to fundamentalism we are faced with a more subtle factor in the process of disintegration within the Christian Religion. That factor is at the heart of Western democracy. It is pseudo-liberalism.

The liberal philosophy of the eighteenth and nineteenth centuries brought enlightenment and progress to both religious and political thought. It enhanced the arts and revived classical taste in poetry and architecture. But a more recent by-product of that philosophy is pseudo-liberalism. It is almost as if would-be liberals have taken to heart Ezra Pound's dictum *make it new* and applied it to every aspect of life—including religion. But to no effect.

Rather than leave alone those things that work, the pseudo-liberal mind is restless unless it initiates change in everything it finds. One feature of this phenomenon is that change becomes accelerated to the point where the institution or tradition can no longer accommodate the means by which change becomes effective. The institution or tradition begins to collapse, necessitating yet more change and so on towards final entropy.

It may seem a little unfair to inveigh against liberalism in this way by relating it to the word 'pseudo'. But even liberalism can be corrupted and I believe it has now become so throughout the whole of our institutional life. We notice, for instance, how those very people who advocate tolerance from within the Church are often the least tolerant members of it. That is because they are not liberals in the right sense at all. A true liberal is not one who responds to every puff of wind and considers progress as the *deus ex machina* to rescue society from stagnation. A liberal is not a thinker who automatically aligns with current opinion, or one who is constantly gazing around trying to find something that is considered to be out of date by the high priests of fashion in order to sweep it away and replace it by *anything* providing it is new. A liberal person is a generous person, whose liberalism is associated with an expansion of the mind, with a broadening of vision, who allows for other views and is not trenchant in position for or against tradition, progress, or even stasis. There are no stock phrases in the liberal vocabulary, no clichés, no strident opinions for or against a cause. Only a love of liberty, which is never surrendered by recourse to violent words or deeds, and a love of truth sustained by learning and humility.

Many recent liturgical changes in the churches have smacked of pseudo-liberalism. Banalities, even vulgarities, have been excused and often encouraged simply because they are a sign in themselves of doing away with tradition. That is not the mark of a well educated liberal.

Chapter 8

Laws, Rules and Bureaucracy

There is a higher law than the Constitution.

William H Seward

The answers to the multifarious problems facing the churches in the West are not easily found. But one problem in particular shows little sign of being resolved. Indeed, all the indications are that it will go on increasing. And this is the inexorable rise in the number of rules and regulations that govern the Institution of Religion. It may be difficult to trace this back to a rational foundation but a clue can be found in a simple formula:

> the weaker the institution the greater its need to establish control by means of bureaucracy.

Now bureaucracy is not the same as administration. The purpose of administration is to serve the institution. In the case of religion that should be to help to promote the religion to hand, by *ad* ministration, leading towards ministry, enabling ministry to take place. It is not apparent in the Church that this is understood.

Good administration is one thing. The proliferation of paperwork, the constant re-visitation of statistical data by checking and double checking, form-filling, direction from the centre by law, rule and regulation to meet every eventuality is quite another.

A test of administration in any organisation is to subtract from that organisation its original purpose and see if the administration is any longer necessary. If it is then it is poor administration. For it has become an end in itself, a bureaucracy in fact. Weak leadership always ends up controlling its organisation by administrative overload, where the original purpose is forgotten, or mislaid, and is replaced by accounting procedures that grow exponentially. Since this is pandemic in our society it would pay to examine briefly how this happens.

Bureaucracy is *centralised* administration. Control by bureaucracy is achieved in two ways. First, the administration asserts itself to the point where without it the institution is not allowed to function. Secondly, it eventually assumes executive power and takes upon itself the authority to direct. This is usually under the guise of budget control, legal directives, auditing advice, and public relations. The rules are then changed from what one should *not* do to what one *should* do. This change of emphasis indicates a move from partial to total control. It marks a departure from liberality.

Once the administration takes on the role of executive the original purpose of the institution has in effect been overthrown and rescue becomes well nigh impossible. There is a feeling, for example, that the Church's obsession with mission statements, usually issued by some bureaucratically directed sector ministry, has nothing to do with mission but simply indicates the fact that the Church is struggling to keep going.

42

Some kind of religion can of course survive within a bureaucratic totalitarianism, but only by artificial means. It then depends upon keeping the people ignorant or fearful. That is when pseudo-liberalism and fundamentalism begin to operate without let or hinder. The Spirit has in effect left and the institution is up for grabs by the most powerful contender—the administrator, the lawyer, the accountant, or one who is expert in press relations in the case of pseudo-liberalism; or intolerance and lack of humour for the fundamentalist. The former leads to dissipation of energy and talent, the latter to the gun and the bomb.

Chapter 9

Government by What?

If the General Synod is at any time dissolved before the fourth year after the last preceding election of the House of Laity or before the fixing of numbers under this rule by the General Synod during that year, the General Synod or the Presidents thereof may give directions with respect to the fixing and certifying of the numbers of members to be elected to the House of Laity by each diocese, and the directions may provide that the numbers so fixed and certified on the last previous occasion shall be deemed to have been fixed and certified for the purpose of the election following the dissolution and the directions may, if the dissolution is known to be impending, be given before it occurs.

Church Representation Rules

The Lord traps the wise in their own cunning.

Proverb

Synodical Government is considered by many to be tantamount to a waste of precious time, a misuse of scarce resources and a profligate abuse of money. The Church of England has taken on this cumbersome and costly machinery of Government by choice. It wishes to be like secular government and

44

has created a bureaucracy accordingly. The means to this end is democracy. But Christianity is not, and never will, be a democracy. Nor is it a business. It is fundamental mistake number one to think it is either or both.

At one time the Parish was the strength of the Church of England. Now the General Synod holds the key to power, sending down to dioceses and parishes items for their agendas, policies to be implemented and the inevitable courses to be attended—all at considerable cost and adding to the already heavy workload of a diminishing number of parish priests and their flocks.

Some parish priests don't mind about this. They love their meetings, courses, conferences. In fact, meetings have become the inexcusable focus of the Church and an excuse for inaction. Without committees the Church of England would flounder, its purpose would be lost. Quite what the point is in the pooling of ignorance in this way one is at a loss to say. But one thing is abundantly clear. With all these meetings and reports, Parochial Church Councils, Synods, Boards of Social Responsibility, Boards of Finance, Bishops' Councils, Archbishops' Councils, the people of England are left utterly unmoved and untouched.

The population at large is in fact bored by what now passes for religion in the National Church. This boredom factor is ignored by the authorities, who think that charging about from one committee to another is somehow doing the Lord's will. Where they do recognise the absence of people but fail to see the cause they presume that the Church of England needs to take on the role of entertainer. It doesn't. It needs to recover its proper role as the communicator of eternal truths.

In the form of an interlude let us think briefly of just a few ways in which the Church of England could begin to save itself. They may not be the answer to decline, or what the people who thirst for true religion are looking for, but they could help to release some of our resources and free the Church to get on with its job. They don't require any sophisticated theology or long deliberations to be effective. They are simply practical solutions.

Chapter 10

Investors in People

...the ministers of God...

The Holy Bible, 2 Corinthians 6: 4

The Church could save considerable time and expense in its dealings with the clergy. This whole matter indicates plainly how the Church has departed from the injunctions and guidelines of Scripture and suffered in consequence. I should like to spend a moment on this at the risk of becoming too particular in the theme.

The Church of England is staffed mainly by clergy men and women. They are known as Vicars, Rectors and Curates, sometimes as ministers. The great majority of them are ordained to the priesthood. Priests are authorised by the Church to minister to congregations and individuals by means of preaching and teaching and in the administration of sacraments. To do this they are expected to undertake certain obligations. For example, they usually have to live in the parish in which they serve.

> Every incumbent must keep residence on his benefice, and in the house of residence (if any) belonging thereto.
>
> K.M. Macmorran, *Cripps on Church and Clergy*

But this has had implications that extend far beyond the niceties of law. It enables clergy to live amongst their parishioners—to get to know them and always to be on hand in times of difficulty.

The link between parish, people and the vicarage or rectory has become legendary down the centuries in the creation of poets, philosophers, naturalists, historians and scholars of all disciplines, adding enormously to the rich, cultural heritage of the nation. And there is perhaps a single over-riding reason behind this. At one time virtually every vicar and rector had freehold. This meant that they owned the house in which they lived as part of their benefice. They did not have to retire. Freehold was for life. But that didn't mean Christian ministers were free to do what they liked. Freehold was, and is, a mark of the freedom of the English Church—and the English people—to have a voice.

There were disadvantages to this system but there were also enormous gains for the Church and Nation. For instance, with freehold a large salary wasn't necessary, for clergy had little need to prepare for retirement except as a matter of choice. Secondly, although there are exceptions, it is generally accepted that to be a good pastor one should be wise, someone who has gained from experience. That takes time, for wisdom tends to increase with age. Another advantage of freehold is that it allows one to speak one's mind. You are independent. Your job does not depend upon currying favour with either your bishop or your parishioners. This can lead to bloody-mindedness, of course. But so what? The Church could do with a few eccentrics. Finally, one important and overlooked factor is the need to mature for leadership. Natural leaders emerge where they are given the time and space to develop. Like a good wine maturing over many years they cannot be rushed. In the secular world it was sixty-five years before Winston Churchill became Prime Minister. He felt that the whole of his life had been a preparation for his huge task. If Moses had had a set career pattern with a cut off point, the Hebrew people would never have made it to the Promised Land.

But the most important point about the Christian priesthood is not the question of privileges and rights, wealth and property, but that it should be based upon Scripture. The peculiar ministry of the Church is founded upon the idea of the Presbyter. The Greek πρεσβύτερος (presbuteros) means 'elder'. It applies to male and female, but the condition is this. The person appointed to the status of presbuteros should literally be an elder, of mature years, which almost certainly means past the age of child rearing. Perhaps the wisdom behind this was to remove the crisis of dual loyalty between one's family and the Church. The Roman Catholic answer to this potential and often unrecognised difficulty has been to introduce, and insist upon, celibacy. In the matter of ministry, however, the Church of England has in effect rejected Scriptural authority and chosen to follow the pattern of secular society.

General Synod introduced obligatory retirement some years ago. This was met with acclaim. The Church was at last being seen to be modernising itself, 'moving into the twentieth century'. The pseudo-liberals had won the day. Behind the issue, though, were several hidden items on the agenda. One was to retire older people from the ministry because they could be considered a stumbling block to reform. Another was to pave the way for diocesan bishops to remove freehold from parishes, to enable them to exercise more control and direction of personnel. But, as with many

49

administrative decisions, this piece of reform work rode roughshod over the rights and interests of the people and led in its own small way to the present plight of the Church.

Synod passed the necessary legislation without making any actuarial computation of what it would cost. Nor did it calculate the effect it would have on the Church and on the clergy themselves. We are now beginning to find out. The costs are astronomical, in the billions, with future pensions now dependent upon freewill offerings by an ageing—and diminishing—churchgoing population. At the time of writing the Church of England has more retired clergy than working clergy. Each one receives a pension and, even with £4.5 billion of assets, the Church is unable properly to fund those pensions. And to cap it all many retired clergy are 'helping out' in parishes up and down the country where the absence of clergy is becoming seriously conspicuous because of the Church's policy of mandatory retirement!

Over the years freehold has been stripped away from parishes, parishes have been joined together, and their vicarages in most cases sold off only to reappear on the market at a later date carrying a grossly increased selling price. And worse, the proceeds from these sales haven't ended up back in the parishes but with the Church Commissioners, who managed to lose nearly a billion pounds of Church funds in the 1990s.

The effect of retiring clergy compulsorily has been to reduce manpower, increase the costs of pensions, replace many vicarages with retirement homes, stretch the available clergy to the point where they are unable to cope, and cause regret in those who have no wish to retire. It has all been smoothed over. The younger clergy may not even be aware of what has happened.

But the final test of whether or not the scheme has been a success is actually to be found amongst the present clergy. They treat their vocation as a career with a *terminus ad quem*. For some the free house provided with the job has ceased to be a privilege. Instead it has become a burden. The poorer clergy see property prices around them rising beyond their reach as the termination of their ministry approaches. People who are elders in age and who wish to offer themselves for the ministry are often denied that prospect. They are considered to be non cost-effective. So much for vocation! The burden on the Church will simply increase beyond its capacity unless the concept of freehold is reintroduced and the retirement age scrapped.

The Church of England could also consider the position of Lay Readers (now called Readers), of whom there are several thousand. They offer their services free to the Church. Each has received considerable training, yet Readers are heavily restricted in the way they can serve. For example, since the Parish Communion movement half a century ago there is a celebration of Holy Communion in most parish churches each week. With the shortage of clergy this places great strain on resources. Yet Readers are not allowed to celebrate Holy Communion! They may not consecrate, pronounce absolution, or bless. This renders them non-operational. The Church could solve the problem overnight by passing a measure to ordain Readers to the priesthood. They could become local priests, licensed to their particular area, or priests to the Church at large. And it wouldn't cost the Church of England an extra penny.

Finally, the Church has to begin to realise once and for all that Bishops, Priests and Deacons do not constitute the only form of ministry in the New Testament. There is another—in Romans chapter 12, and 1 Corinthians 12. Here we find the ideal of a Church constituted by ordinary people who exercise the gifts of the Spirit—wisdom, knowledge, faith, healing &c—with no salary and with no reference to the priesthood at all. In Ephesians chapter 4 there is a description of the ministry of the early Church.

> Some to be apostles, some prophets, some evangelists, some pastors and teachers, to equip God's people for work in his service, to the building up of the body of Christ.
>
> *The Holy Bible (NEB)*, Ephesians 4: 11

Surely the ideal way ahead is a combination of all these models based upon the ministry of Christ and his disciples—one main church in an area, with its freehold and full time priest; twelve daughter churches with their locally ordained, unpaid ministers; and the whole laity empowered *to be* the Church in the exercise of their own personal ministries. The Church of England shows little sign that it is prepared to launch into the deep in this fashion. There are too many vested interests to protect. The preferred option is the career pattern of the world.

With all its initiatives, experiments, and schemes for the ministry, the bureaucratically run Church has surrendered itself to secular ways and paid a high price for it. The early Church, with a handful of people, minimal structure and few buildings—and with a fraction of the pro rata budget of today—managed to convert the entire Roman Empire!

Chapter 11

Disestablishment?

What constitutes a state?

Sir William Jones, *Ode in Imitation of Alcaeus*

Another chestnut in the life of the Church of England is Establishment. Amongst other things 'establishment' means:

> the form of religion and church government established by law in any country; the established church of a country.

The Encyclopaedic Dictionary

To some degree all religions are established. Islam is possibly one of the most firmly established religions in the world. To be established a religion has to be politically recognised by a nation and hold an official and protected place in that nation's affairs. Establishment can of course vary in its form and content. It can even be part of a secular state. It is, for instance, almost inconceivable that Israel could formally separate itself from the Jewish Faith even though it may claim to be a non-religious State. The American Constitution includes the following amendment under the Bill of Rights:

53

> Congress shall make no law respecting an
> establishment of religion, or prohibiting the free
> exercise thereof; or abridging the freedom of
> speech, or of the press; or the right of the people
> peaceably to assemble, and to petition the
> Government for a redress of grievances.

Article I

A *particular* Faith therefore cannot be part of the constitution of the United States, but *all* are as a consequence of the right held by its citizens to exercise the freedom of choice. In other words religion itself is implicitly acknowledged by the State.

The Church of England is quite different. The Church here is almost inextricably intertwined with the State, the Monarchy and Parliament. Indeed, the Church of England is based upon the principle of royal supremacy, which is not without precedent in Scripture.

> Submit yourselves to every ordinance of man for
> the Lord's sake: whether it be to the king, as
> supreme; Or unto governors...

The Holy Bible, 1 Peter 2: 13,14

In the past, establishment has proved to be a strength. Its weakness is in the assumption that the Church is here to stay, and therefore is a familiar piece of the national structure which requires neither settlement nor sacrifice.

I was once sitting at lunch with a member of the Shadow Cabinet who proudly declared that he was entirely in favour of disestablishment. When I asked why he felt like this, he replied that he didn't see why he should formally have to acknowledge a Church that

54

continually meddled in politics. The Church, he said, seems to mind everyone else's business but its own!

Establishment *is* political, however. Perhaps that is why, in the face of enormous demographic pressures, some members of the Church of England admit they too would welcome disestablishment. But if they think that here lies the solution to all the problems facing Christendom today they are mistaken. The legal disentanglement alone would take many years and serve further to take the mind of the Church away from its primary task, which is not to be established or disestablished nor to remind others of their business in thinly veiled political agendas, but to be a pure instrument of faith and grace. In addition to this deflection from purpose the process of disestablishment would be a financial disaster. It is estimated that the Church of England would lose up to a third of its assets if it went ahead. And at the end of the day what difference would it make? Would we have higher quality clergy and bishops? Would the organisation be pared down, a new thrust of interest in religion emerge?

The arguments for or against establishment are simply too ill defined and too luxurious to justify in these crucial times. There are plenty of other ways in which the Church can get its house in order, as we shall see. In the meantime, it is important that leaders and members of this once great institution have the courage to recognise that there is a problem and that it will not go away by ignoring it or nodding at it. What should now be occupying the minds of the hierarchy is something more important than the survival of the institution of the Church, established or disestablished. It is the very survival of Christianity in all its forms.

Chapter 12

The Hope of Salvation?

From the dust of creeds out-worn.

Percy Bysshe Shelley, *Prometheus Unbound*

The great Christian theologian St Augustine of Hippo wrote:

There is no salvation outside the Church.

His words echoed those of St Cyprian a century earlier:

There cannot be salvation for any, except in the Church.

The sentiments of both these writers could now be inverted. Rather than the Church—and the word is used here as a collective noun for all Christian churches—being seen as the means of salvation, it stands in need of salvation itself. Salvation consists partly in how we respond to Life. And Life is beyond religion. The Church must now *include* itself in the drama of Christianity, therefore, rather than simply be a commentator or facilitator on its behalf. It isn't entitled any more to be playwright, director, actor and prompt.

For many years the churches have been talking about unity between them. But they have proved that such unity is as far away as ever, in spite of the Lord's own prayer 'that they all may be one' (John 17: 21). Why, Christians cannot even share the most precious focal point of communion, the Eucharist. Anglicans worshipping in Roman Catholic churches, for example, are barred from partaking in the sacrament. There are instances of shared ministry between non-conformist churches and the Church of England but for the most part these are merely tokens put forward to keep the ecumenical movement alive or to reduce running costs.

Disunity in Christendom does little to promote the idea of God as the One who stands behind redemption, reconciliation and unity. Churches that meant business would long ago have abandoned their cul-de-sac mentality and thrust into a new age with truly inspiring steps forward—a common sacramental practice, a united ministry, and a glory in distinction, variety and adventure. By contrast, the churches present themselves as being dyed-in-the-wool, vague and reactionary in some quarters, whilst in others they lack dignity, serenity and gravitas as their members leap about in worship like performers in a circus act, or seek out lost souls like prowling panthers.

The Church's claim to hold the key to salvation can commend itself only on the following conditions: that there is authentic unity throughout Christendom; that this unity is experienced at all levels in friendliness, co-operation and generosity of heart; that it is expressed through common beliefs and practices in the very fields founded by Christ himself—the Gospel, the Ministry and the Sacraments. Where differences occur they would be accepted and absorbed into the unity.

These conditions have never been met.

Chapter 13

Is Redemption Possible?

By the term 'chaos' we mean the complicated, unpredictable, seemingly random behavior of a system.

James T Cushing, *Philosophical Concepts in Physics*

We are nearing the end of our critical observations and have seen clearly that, in spite of areas of great goodness within it, the Church stands in need of some radical changes. So the question arises: is it possible for the Church to meet its self-confessed challenge? Yes, but only by accepting what it has done *to* the name of Christ and not simply what it imagines it does *for* the name of Christ can the Church hope for a future. For such would be the measure of its truthfulness and humility.

Within the Church there are many good, thoughtful and sincere Christians who bring credit to the Faith, who persevere silently in their troubles and bestow a grace upon human life and respect for the world around them. There are lovely communities of believing Christians who faithfully go about their business without seeking reward or favour. With these we have no quarrel—simply admiration and humble gratitude. In recent times, though, and in certain branches of the Church, the Person of Christ has been brought low, denigrated even in some cases, by activist Christians who strive to be relevant, acceptable and political. But the experiment has failed. The 'Jesus movement' has attracted too many sectarian minds who seem to be incapable of thinking high thoughts, and who scorn any attempts to introduce an interpretation of Scripture that coincides with the deepest reflections of the human mind. Truly the Lord's name is being taken in vain by some of the antics and presumptions of those who call themselves Christians. Why?

At one time it could well have been argued that the Church of England was far too academic, its theology pedantic and male orientated. In recent years, though, the pendulum has swung the other way. The Church has gradually become *anti*-intellectual, and accordingly has helped to create a damaging climate of moral and spiritual relativism. It has also become anti-traditional, cutting adrift from the continuity of the past and allowing itself to float on the seas of media coverage and popular opinion. This has resulted in a ceaseless exercise of personal propaganda and an unseemly indulgence in sentiment and feeling. It is pitiful to witness the clergy of the Church striving to entertain their congregations with any device that springs readily to hand. I have heard of a clergyman taking services wearing swimming trunks and skating on a surf board down the aisle, another dressed up as a clown riding a one-wheeled bike. All very amusing stuff no doubt. But its relevance? The sacred deserves better—and so do the people.

The loss of transcendence is accompanied by an almost overbearing sense of familiarity. Bishops, academics and clergy talk nowadays as if they know intimately the mind of God on any number of subjects—war, sex, economics, politics, the future... I often wonder when I hear people use such words as 'we believe in a God who...' whether they really are aware of the vastness of the universe around them, a universe that extends well beyond the domestic affairs of the human race.

Having failed to find in the Scriptures a precedent for its pseudo-liberal tendencies, the Church now rejects the rational foundations of those Scriptures and neatly and expediently identifies what is morally right with the way the majority of people behave—its motive, perhaps, being to win popularity with minimum cost to itself and the avoidance of embarrassment in the world. In so doing it has displaced, foolishly, much of the New Testament that speaks of the eternal, the beyond, the transcendent and the cosmic nature of religion as a whole, replacing the universality and grandeur of the original Christian Faith with a particularised worldliness that rings hollow at a time when increasing numbers of people are reaching out to the heavens for their inspiration. For them it doesn't matter any more what the Church thinks or does. In striving to become relevant the Church has ended up being almost entirely irrelevant.

In fact, with its emphasis on organisation, finance and law, the Church of England in particular is now so identified with the spirit of the age that it runs the risk of a take-over by an already over-regulated world of politics and economics. The freedoms for which the Church has fought down the centuries are being readily handed over to the secular state, not by force this time but through the adoption of a subtle and apparently innocuous political programme to which many churchgoers innocently subscribe—human rights, equal opportunities, non-discrimination and rules of employment. The consequences of this failure of nerve have not yet been calculated. But we are beginning to see the signs and portents.

The seeds of decay of Institutional Christianity were sown long ago. Only now have those seeds grown into flourishing weeds. There are two prevalent responses. The first is like the gardener who cannot distinguish a weed from a plant on the one hand and who rejoices in everything that grows in the garden on the other. This is indiscriminate liberalism and is quite deadly. It is usually protected by inherited wealth, either privately or institutionally, and is often accompanied by personal indifference. It represents the position of many within the Church at the present time. The other response is like the gardener who is overwhelmed by the task in hand and walks away in despair. Such despair is corrosive. This is often the attitude of those who have given up on the Church altogether. Neither response is commendable.

I believe that only a long hard look at the central issues now confronting the religions of humankind will enable us to avert cataclysmic disaster. That long hard look may have to include the unthinkable. If Christianity is to survive and flourish it may be necessary to sever its links with organised religion altogether. Or at least the Church should cease to have *control* over the Christian Faith and all those who call themselves Christians, and take on a new role— perhaps that of custodian trustee. It is no longer possible to confine the Spirit to the limits of the institution.

I refer to the quotation at the beginning of this chapter. What is true of chaos in physics is equally true in matters of religion. We are in a state of chaos and the very randomness of the situation today compels me to be bold and make the following declaration:

The hour has come for Christ to be rescued from the grip of the institutional churches—to be restored to his rightful place as the living symbol of the reality behind all things.

And, further, God must be saved from the demise of organised religion—and be delivered, as is his due, into the glorious mystery of Being.

I am not calling for an end to organised religion but for a sense of transcendence amongst individual Christians as well as those who seek truth outside the Church. The truly religious person, whilst acknowledging what the churches have to offer, must have the confidence to rise above the shackles of institutionalism and develop a personal responsibility for faith. We can no longer afford to allow the Church to do our spirituality for us.

Are we courageous enough to begin again and put behind us those feeble attempts of the modern Church to win the world by changing its image? Are we bold enough to redefine our spiritual fellowship, re-examine the foundations of Faith, search the Scriptures for hidden truths and explore the potential for a personal religion—a religion that extends beyond the boundaries of the Church, yet which in the end may be its salvation?

Part Two

Religious Truth

Chapter 14

There *is* Hope for Religion, but...

*We have just enough religion to make us hate, but
not enough to make us love one another.*

Jonathan Swift, *Thoughts on Various Subjects*

The events of September 11th 2001 in New York
and Washington caused many people to question
the minds behind the appalling deeds witnessed
live on television by many millions of people. How
could anyone fly an aircraft, fully laden with innocent
people, into a tower block occupied at the time by
thousands of workers going about their lawful business?

The whole event was a tragic metaphor. With the
collapse of the two towers of the World Trade Centre it
was as though a certain order had come to an end. And
indeed it had. The terrorist attack on America—aimed
at economic, military and democratic targets—marked
for the whole world the final moments of an old era
and the beginning of the new. But, even long after
the event, people are not clear about what the
characteristics of this new era will be.

At about the same time as the attack in America there
were uncomfortable scenes in Northern Ireland as

Protestants shouted abuse at little Catholic children going to school. A bomb was thrown. Children wept. People throughout the world felt ashamed. That too was a metaphor.

Now what did these two apparently dissociated events have in common, and what do they indicate about the state of the world? Simply this. They were both associated with religion. Although there were protestations to the contrary it was in the name of Allah that the hijackers forced the crews off their flight decks and steered those aircraft into an absolute catastrophe for the whole world. It was people of the Protestant faith who stood shouting at the tiny children in Belfast.

Neither religion responded with the dignity of refutation that one should expect. It follows that each of the two events indicates a seismic shift in the way that religion can now quite justifiably be viewed. Things cannot continue as they have been.

At every level, from the ruling bodies of religious institutions right down to the ordinary believer, Church people and members of different faiths simply cannot continue to smooth over the wrong-doings of the miscreants in their midst simply by condemning them publicly by formula and declaring that religions are not really like that. They are. The plain fact is that there is an official view, which comes from within religion and is often based upon what *ought* to be the case, and there is the view of reason based upon observation of what actually is the case. These two views do not coincide. People are falling out all over the place in the name of religion. They cannot agree on church committees, for instance, about the most trivial issues. They deny the truths of religion at every turn as they argue about the various banal matters that religion puts on its agenda.

66

There is a level of awkwardness, lack of openness to new ideas and a deep resistance to truth throughout the Church. We all like everything to be as it was, or as we think it should be. As one wit put it, we don't mind change providing it doesn't make any difference. Opinion is counted far more than objectivity. In other religions, opinions are hardening into obsession. Trouble is looming. So what is the conclusion? Could it be that *the old order of religion is coming to an end?*

Chapter 15

Religion is an Institution

His religion, at best, is an anxious wish; like that
of Rabelais, "a great Perhaps".

Thomas Carlyle, *Burns*

Religion in some form or other has been part of the human psyche for a very long time, in fact ever since human life first peered out at the world from the security of caves. The major religions, of course, were founded in comparatively recent times—Hinduism, Judaism and Buddhism several centuries before Christ, Islam several centuries after Christ.

In spite of being separated by hundreds of years, there are certain identifiable and common factors in all these religions. One is the creation and use of Scripture. The Scriptures are writings gathered together over a period of time under the title 'Sacred' or 'Holy'. The Holy Scriptures are characterised by their reference to sacred or holy events, events relating to mystical and spiritual phenomena. They usually portray truths by means of allusion or by storytelling and are often written in the form of proverbs, maxims and sayings of wise teachers. Thus the Jews have the Torah, the Buddhists writings such as the Dhammapada. The

Hindus have the Vedas, the Upanishads, and the Bhagavad Gita, the Muslims their Koran, Christians the Gospels. These Scriptures are considered to be inspired, the truths contained within them revealed.

Another feature shared by the major religions is that they all have holy buildings—synagogues, temples, mosques or churches. Each religion builds its own House of God, with its focal point of altar or shrine. Within these buildings worship of the Gods takes place with elaborate ritual and ceremony. Usually the rituals and ceremonies are set out in formal books of worship.

Finally, no religion would be complete without a priesthood or professional body of people who are placed in charge of the Scriptures, the shrines and the acts of worship. These clerics are given authority over the people and make pronouncements in the name of their religion and Gods.

And so it has been for thousands of years. Religion has gradually become organised into an Institution with its formularies, doctrines, priesthoods, sacred buildings and Scriptures. These points of common ground should bind the religions together but in fact they do not. They become the focus of disagreement, between the religions and within them. There is only one casualty here and that is—Truth.

Chapter 16

When Truth is Possessed

Let there be truth between us.

Goethe

A
s each religion has organised itself around the various cornerstones of its own codified belief it has become inclusive for its members but exclusive to the rest. And here is the supreme paradox which only religion itself can hope to overcome.

In the name of its God and revealed Scripture each religion claims to have the truth. And not only does it claim to have the truth, it maintains that the other religions do not have the truth. Indeed religions are so convinced that they are in unique possession of the truth that they are prepared to go to war with other religions about it. Much of the world's folly is based upon this misunderstanding.

There is no greater cause of division in human affairs than the confusion of truth with falsehood. And there is no greater cause of falsehood than to believe that truth is a personal possession. If truth is considered to be a personal possession it is no surprise to find that the truth appears to differ according to which religion we choose.

Out of all the religions in the world, though, which is right? Not all can be right if each religion claims to be unique in knowing the truth, and, in so claiming, holds that others do not know the truth. Perhaps all religions possess an aspect of the truth? And further, perhaps these aspects, when added together, equate with the truth about God? But if this is true, why do religions spend so much energy in refuting each other? An argument is not made correct by arguing that others are not correct. Similarly a belief is not made true simply by believing that other beliefs are false.

It is surprising that no one in the field of religion seems to carry the fault line to its natural conclusion. And the conclusion is this. If each religion, in turn, is right in thinking that all other religions are wrong then all religions must be wrong. That is the logical result of exclusivity, and is leading to a widespread rejection of religion *per se* by many independent thinking minds.

> In religion,
> What damned error, but some sober brow
> Will bless it and approve it with a text,
> Hiding the grossness with fair ornament?

> William Shakespeare, *The Merchant of Venice,*
> III.ii.77

Truth cannot be divided into self-contradictory parts, and dressing religion up in various guises cannot disguise this fact.

Chapter 17

Religious Correction

Increase in us true religion.

The Book of Common Prayer, Collect, Trinity 7

When you believe that truth is on your side it is so easy to bypass humility and enter into judgement. One of the greatest tragedies of religion is that its judgements are almost always in the negative key. Of course that in itself is a negative statement! But there is much in religion that requires the attention of a critical mind. Eventually, however, negation has to give way to something more positive.

The phrase *contra mundum* means 'against the world' and it is in this spirit that religion is perceived whenever religious authority pronounces on anything, whether it is economics, politics, or society at large. The Church, for instance, seems to assume to itself a divine right to judge others, but forgets that Christ's injunction was not to judge lest we in turn be judged— and no doubt be found wanting. As the text says:

> All have sinned, and come short of the glory of God.

> *The Holy Bible*, Romans 3: 23

72

What is this insatiable desire in religious people to correct others, to remind them that they are wrong? Could it be traced back to the concept of divine judgement? If the Church or any other institutional form of religion sees itself as the instrument of God's grace, it doesn't require a huge logical step or imaginative leap for that institution to believe it is the instrument of God's power, especially in correcting the world from its folly. Indeed, over the years the Church has considered itself to be the instrument not only of grace and power but of torture and calculated death. Some religions continue this role in our present time. Fatwahs and jihads are the order of the day in certain Islamic countries. Punishment by death is the penalty meted out by religious authorities for even the most meagre of crimes. Hinduism and Buddhism are not exempt from administering the rule of punitive law either, making religion altogether appear to be a vicious and revengeful code of social correction rather than the repository of peace, virtue and tolerance.

It is my firm belief that something must be wrong not only with the world, therefore, but with religions in their present form. And I also believe that the sense of retributive power within the religions comes from a false assumption about the nature of God.

Chapter 18

Tribal Gods

We are all embarked on a sea of troubles.

Latin proverb

Only by recognising the common ground between religions can religions hope in the long term to serve the truth.

The protraction of false religion is not our concern here. False religion arises wherever the higher order of truth is sacrificed for the lower orders of narrow Scriptural interpretation, institutional bigotry, priestly functionalism, bureaucratic power and the concept of a particularised God.

What do I mean by a particularised God? I mean the God of Islam, the God of the Jews, the Christian God, the Gods of the Hindus—a God *of the tribe*. Not the God of the universe, of space and time, the God of heaven and earth, but a God constructed in our own image, who belongs *to us and to nobody else*.

The inevitable consequence of a particularised God and a narrowly defined religion is division. But such division plays no part in the pursuit of truth. The idea of two opposing armies of Christians and Muslims, for instance, charging towards each other with nihilistic ferocity, each shouting threats in the name of their own

God, is ludicrous. So is the notion that churches in the same village or town can somehow be in competition. Truth is not decided like that. Whenever we hear a speaker on *Thought for the Day* talking about their own personal God we know something is wrong. We do not speak, for example, about our own personal universe except by reference to our selves.

This idea of God has now to be seriously revised, even abolished altogether, if we are to escape from the many misjudgements that arise between religions and allow the proper definitions of God, reality and the universe to prevail.

Chapter 19

Tradition or Change?

We should not worry ourselves about things
which are past.

Napoleon I

The truths of religion are usually enshrined in Scripture. But if they are to be useful to humankind they must extend beyond the confines of particular religions. In one sense, of course, the truths of Scripture can exist in a state of timelessness.

> Better is a little with righteousness than great revenues with injustice.
>
> *The Holy Bible (RSV),* Proverbs 16: 8

The human truth of such a text does not belong to a certain period of history. It is for all time.

But in another sense the process of time allows us to unravel layers of meaning and truth which previous generations did not explore. This ambiguous relation between ancient tradition and modernity is reflected in the problem that constantly faces poetry—of writing in the here and now for the there and then. The problem is expressed by Ali Ahmed Said, the Arabic poet:

76

> Therefore it became clear to me that modernity
> was both of time and outside time: of time
> because it is rooted in the movement of history, in
> the creativity of humanity, coexisting with man's
> striving to go beyond the limitations which
> surround him; and outside time because it is
> a vision which includes in it all times and cannot
> only be recorded as a chronological event.

Adonis, *An Introduction to Arab Poetics*

What is true of modernity should also apply to tradition. But traditions can ossify. And where ossified traditions are founded upon the avoidance of historical continuity, or upon narrow translations from one thought pattern to another, errors are perpetuated. The Russian-born philosopher Ouspensky put it well:

> Truths that become old become decrepit and
> unreliable; sometimes they may be kept going
> artificially for a certain time, but there is no life in
> them.

P D Ouspensky, *A New Model of the Universe*

In spite of the fact that the religious spirit is very much alive in many places, organised religions throughout the world have reached a state of ossification. They no longer serve the purpose they once had. This phenomenon happened in the first few centuries of Christianity and again in the Middle Ages, when doctrinal rigidity forced religions apart ever more widely, introducing the concept of the infidel and extending that of heretic. It happened in the sixteenth century as Christendom split into separate traditions. It is happening today. Schism, sectarianism and funda-mentalism have their roots in traditions that have

77

become corrupted through a refusal on the part of religious institutions to recognise the truth *about* themselves whilst at the same time claiming to be sole possessors of the truth *for* themselves.

Chapter 20

A Warning from the Past

That great dust-heap called "history".

Augustine Birrell, *Obiter Dicta,* 'Carlyle'

The next stage is what matters. Some religions in the past have collapsed. The hieroglyphic religions of ancient Egypt are now the object of fascinating enquiry, but they remain buried in the Valley of the Kings and their artefacts are on display in the museums of Cairo and Luxor. Temples covering vast acres lie in ruins on the banks of the Nile. Elsewhere, the world is littered with the archaeological remains of religions that have fallen into desuetude.

Few people, if any, actually follow those religions today. The organic unity of the buildings, the Scriptures, the priests, has long since departed in the cycle of history. So it may well be with the religions of our own time. No doubt many in the ancient world believed their religions would continue forever. There are similar assurances given in the contemporary world. The idea that St Paul's Cathedral, Westminster Abbey and Notre Dame may one day lie in ruins is beyond imagination. So it was for those people who contemplated the living temples of Edfu, Esna and Abu Simbel. As the paintings of David Roberts in the

nineteenth century show, most of them were until
recently half hidden under the desert. Without the
archaeological percipience of Victorian explorers they
would probably have been lost forever under the sands
of time. That is the way religions can go. They
develop their own momentum of growth but also of
decline.

What, if anything, can arrest that decline? The short
answer is that if something extra to religion is required
in order to stimulate it and prevent its deterioration then
the religion itself is wanting. That is the case with
European Christianity at present. At one time
Christianity was strong enough to create its own mores
and spiritual values. It has, however, been the tendency
of liberalism over the years to absorb into the
infrastructures of the Church secular values which in
the end makes the Church indistinguishable from the
world around it. This in no small part has caused the
present crisis.

> There is a crisis of values which even politics and
> the media have got hold of because the customer
> is worried about his security, his privacy and his
> death—which is all the more unacceptable
> because it has been deferred. This crisis of
> values, which even the rationalists have called by
> its proper name, is the crisis of the churches, or,
> better, the crisis of the Church. The Church crisis
> is not the crisis of Protestantism or Catholicism, it
> is a crisis common to all churches. Protestant
> churches, faithful, unfortunately, to their vocation
> of being the vanguard, have only been affected
> sooner and more deeply than the others,
> especially the Catholic Church which is rudely
> shaken in its European domains.

> *The Reformation* edited by Pierre Chaunu

80

I suspect that this is true of all major religions. As for the Christian Church it needs nothing less than a revival of spirit. And this will only come about by a radical re-formation of its beliefs, its way of life and its structures.

> To the extent that the Reformed tradition sees itself as purifying the approach to and reception of the ancient tradition, it carried within itself the promise of new reformations. Thus churches which issued from the Reformation soon found themselves called to produce a new reformation, a new Apostolic age—we have witnessed it— called the Revival.

ibid.

The dynamic of renewal is both reflective and prophetic. Too much reflection, looking back to the past and imitating its forms of belief and action, only leads to fossilisation. But an institution that throws away everything to do with past beliefs in order to start again becomes merely revolutionary, that is, revolves, without any necessary forward movement. A prophetic religion on the other hand creates a dynamic intention which is fulfilled only by hard work, courage, and a sense of perseverance that is initiated by hope.

The first requirement for a Church or religion to be reflective *and* prophetic is to develop an honest recognition of truth. To deny fact is to debilitate the mind for future action. Upbeat statements in the face of decline, loss or negation are not only misleading, they are duplicitous. When they are made by leaders who are charged with responsibility to lead people through the negative and out of their loss those leaders are party to the cause of further decline. For they have usurped their privilege of being called to share the burden of hope. Realism can never be equated with false hope, nor with the desire for ease of mind. It recognises things as they are.

> Complacency can be bought too cheaply by denying the importance of empty churches, the quest for pleasure, immersion in the present, capitulation before nothingness, emptiness and the abandonment of action, discourse and thought. All of these are signs of an absolute rupture which it is absurd to deny.

ibid.

Realists don't pretend that it isn't dark when it is. They bring their own light to banish the darkness.

Part Three

The Modern Mind

Chapter 21

In the Depths of Religion

The old order changeth, yielding place to new,
And God fulfils Himself in many ways,
Lest one good custom should corrupt the world.

Alfred, Lord Tennyson, *Morte d'Arthur*

The realist faces the fact that rather than being the answer to the world's problems religion can easily be seen to be a major contributor to them. The inchoate formlessness of contemporary spirituality has finally revealed the incapacity of each religion to extend beyond its own self-imposed limitations. It follows that religion is at present incapable of solving the human condition of fragmentation because it is in a state of fragmentation itself. Nothing can be a source of healing, peace and truth if it promotes separation, disagreement and falsehood.

The desolate state of humankind in many areas of the world in its poverty, oppression and conflict could well have been relieved by a true and beautiful image of God. But the means of deliverance is no longer clear. The spirit of transcendence, once proclaimed and followed by serious and devout adherents to truth, has somehow been lost between the temples of public influence and the inner sanctum of private belief. Thus it is possible to charge the world's religions that in their apparent animosity of spirit towards one another and in holding on to their jealously guarded preserves they express not only a universal desolation but an absence of hope for humankind. We can also say, with some justification, that collectively they have played a large part in the downfall of God.

Chapter 22

The Absent God

A God denies, my friend...

Horace, *Epodes*

The loss of a creative vision, especially in the context of disunity between institutional religions, is the tragedy of our times. In every home, in every village and city we are destroying the roots and continuity of society because we lack a proper foundation. The world seems to be led by advocates of change, fashion and trend in the West and by reactionary forces in the East. The two are on collision course.

In the present climate of war and murmurings of war—often in the name of this religion or that—the very foundations of life are under question. And behind our loss of direction in human affairs there is the phenomenon of what could be termed the 'displacement of God'.

In the West the existence of an omnipotent and righteous God, author and authority of life, founder of all that exists and all that is noble, just and true, can no longer be taken for granted. God speaks no more to the people. Of course the *word* 'God' is used, as often perhaps as it ever was. But the point must now be made that God, as religions portray him, has become almost a void in human intellect and experience. In its divided state institutionalised religion has seriously damaged the identity of God. And it is because it unwittingly serves to *dis*integrate God that it surrenders its authority to console and inspire humankind as a whole.

Religions and their articles of belief still attract human sentiment, of course. Many people, often with the best intentions, hold on doggedly to beliefs which have lost their hold on the rest of the world. Some go through the motions of religious ceremony and practice as if acting the same scene of a play over and over again. It seems that out of respect for an idea whose final moment has come they continue to believe in the idea for fear of the consequences if they don't. But what they represent sadly fails to satisfy the increasing numbers in humankind who seek an objective under-standing of truth.

What is undeniable is that some people are guided by a genuine faith, a care for others and a sincere love for humankind that results in noble and self-sacrificing deeds. There are many beautiful lives devoted to making this world a better place for all. But it is still right to say that if we are to find the truth in an infinite and ever changing universe we must acknowledge that the truth of existence itself is ineluctably a wider concept than is the God of religion.

Chapter 23

A Secular Society

*Where is your wise man now, your man of
learning, or your subtle debater—limited, all of
them, to this passing age?*

The Holy Bible (NEB), 1 Corinthians 1: 20

There is one deep-rooted reason why religion in
the West is in decline. Not only has it lost touch
with the people, and divided itself into
irreconcilable units, it has allowed its relations with
science to diminish to the point where scientific method
has left religion in a wilderness.

At one time religion was the source of inspiration to
the arts and the sciences. Indeed, theology was known
as the queen of the sciences. The remarkable
development of knowledge, the flourishing of art,
music, sculpture, architecture and poetry during and
after the medieval age was due in no small part to the
belief systems of that time. There was a supreme vision
of the universe into which every aspect of human
knowledge fitted and received its seal of approval.

Until quite recently society has always been located
on a religious map. But this map and its reference
points have been removed. Direction finding has now
become much more difficult. People are disorientated

and are looking for other kinds of map on which to locate their position. Once they become comfortable with a particular form of cartography they will see little reason to change again.

Religion has yet to wake up to the fact that the map of today is secular, its co-ordinates those of time and space—in other words, of science. In the past few decades human knowledge has tended to focus on the finite dimensions of space-time to the exclusion of anything which does not fall within a strictly empirical criterion. According to this bench-mark for what passes as true knowledge, meaning and truth can be obtained only from what is calculated or observed. What you see is what you get.

Clearly, within this criterion religion fails the test. You can see and touch material things. Therefore they exist. You cannot do the same with God. You can prove things mathematically, but you cannot prove the existence of God. The fact that we use the term 'God' doesn't imply that the term stands for something outside the conceptual frame of thought.

This inherent difficulty in proving that non-conceptual reality extends beyond space-time leads many people to have doubts about the existence of God. For since the concept of God and the idea of spirituality cannot be thought of as the conclusion of logical deduction or the result of direct observation, they are dismissed out of hand. Consequently the whole structure of religion collapses into a state of non-meaning. So it's really all a question of belief—or opinion. Is it surprising, therefore, that God has ceased to be central to people's lives? The secular mind and religious belief do not make comfortable travelling companions.

It is going to be exceedingly difficult to replace the secular map by anything that is remotely religious. The reference points, the scale, the grid and the contours are now firmly grounded in forms of existence that reject the traditional means by which human beings once found their bearings and set their course through life.

Here then is an important part of the background to the religious doubt that prevails today. The powerful influence of secular thought has had an overwhelming effect on the Western mind, and although we are recovering a sense of equilibrium and allowing that certain kinds of knowledge do not fit into a rigid empirical framework yet nevertheless remain valid, the effect on religion has been devastating, leading many thinkers within religion to give up the struggle to go beyond a secular brief. For them, too, God is no longer an objective reality.

Religions now need an upheaval to shake them out of their sure repose. Not only should they guard more resolutely against fundamentalism, superstition and pseudo-liberalism, they should also be prepared to answer the onslaught of deep scientific enquiry about the truths that religions themselves claim to hold if they are to regain the credibility they once had.

Chapter 24

A Theological Response

*In the Religion of Being everything is brought
down into time, into transience.*

Don Cupitt, *The Revelation of Being*

The purpose of religion is not to create God out
of faith but to do the very opposite. Its true
purpose is actually to define God in such a way
as to make the non-existence of God impossible. If we
are going to try to understand what we mean by the
term 'God', however, we need to put the term into
context. This context can be at different levels of our
understanding—the universe of space-time, the heavens,
reality or eternity.

According to the Cambridge theologian Don Cupitt,
we should not concern ourselves with a vision of life
beyond the temporal. He suggests that 'there are no
substances, and no eternal truths'.

> In the older philosophies and in classical theism
> one found final intellectual satisfaction and
> happiness in the vision of something that was
> eternal and perfect, and logically *had* to be what it
> was. One was taken up into the Infinite. The
> human spirit could not finally be content with

anything less than eternal necessity and absolute
perfection of being. So it was from Parmenides to
Hegel. But now I am saying that we can and must
find the same eternal happiness here and now, and
in the vision of everything as being only
contingent, only finite, only temporal and
'perishing' and outsideless.

Don Cupitt, *The Revelation of Being*

There is a certain attraction in what Cupitt says, but if
he is right in suggesting that space-time is all that there
is then the future of God seems bleak. In Cupitt's
world all our propositions about this God—and our
associated beliefs too—become meaningless. The word
'God' now refers not to an objective reality but to
a mere construction in our minds. The reality of 'God'
is limited to a psychological condition which expresses
itself in our interpretation of the world around us.

People do not articulate their doubts about the
validity of religious statements in quite this way but
they do share a sceptical point of view when it comes to
the consideration of religion and its claims to truth. For
them Cupitt's position simply represents the end of the
line for conventional religious belief. A faith that
depends solely upon the veridical authority of Scripture
is like a currency that has lost its value.

Cupitt isn't speaking here directly about God, of
course, but about the conditions under which the term
'God' is to be accepted or not. It is those conditions
that we must explore before we can address the ultimate
question—*does* God exist?

Part Four

The Search for God

Chapter 25

What *is* Religion?

If I rest, I rust.

Martin Luther

It is time to begin again. The world's religions in their present form may survive, perhaps for hundreds of years, but they will go on losing credibility if their present strategy of self preservation and exclusivity continues to be enacted on the world's stage. They have, as they say colloquially but accurately, largely lost the plot. What matters now is not what separates or divides religions but what, if anything, brings them together in a common purpose. Indeed the moment has come for us to ask some fundamental questions. What *is* the purpose of religion? Is its presence any longer necessary for a world whose definitions derive mainly from a secular construction of morals, science and politics? And can human beings pursue religious truth without having to run the gauntlet of religion in its institutional form?

The original meaning of the word 'religion' in the Western world was twofold: to bind together (Latin: *religare*), and to be in a state of awe and wonder about the nature of the universe (Latin: *religio*). At their purest the Scriptures point humankind in this direction,

97

but we have to accept that institutionalised religion seldom achieves these high ideals. The first question to be faced in the reconstruction of religion is why are religions, most of whom purport to be the instruments of peace and repositories of truths about God, always at loggerheads with each other? Perhaps the answer is in the very foundations of the religions themselves.

Chapter 26

Truth Revealed

*And to make all men see what is the fellowship of
the mystery, which from the beginning of the
world hath been hid in God.*

The Holy Bible, Ephesians 3: 9

The major religions claim that our knowledge of
God or knowledge about God can come about
only through a form of revelation, which then
passes into tradition. But how do we verify what is
claimed to be revealed? An obscure eighteenth-century
clergyman sums up the position:

> Here we are to enquire, first, how we come to
> believe the Truth of *Matters of Fact* recorded in
> the Bible. Secondly, supposing the Truth of the
> History, how it appears that the Matters recorded
> are of *divine Revelation*, and that the Doctrine
> came from God. This seems to be the most
> rational and proper Method of coming to a true
> Judgement in this Matter.
>
> David Collyer, *Collyer on the Bible*

Revelation may have been a satisfactory route to God
for many generations past but in recent years it has
largely lost its appeal. The word 'revelation' glows no

more for a generation bred in the manners of investigative science or the plain pragmatism of human behaviour. It certainly cannot constitute a *proof* for the existence of God. Nor can a definition of God consist in the tabulation of characteristics which we might claim to know through revelation. Conversely, we are not at liberty to decide by means of revelation that there is a God and then choose what sort of characteristics this God shall have. Yet that is how religions would prefer it to be.

Tradition based upon revelation tends to leave human beings in the passive state. Look at what happens in many of our religious buildings for instance. Congregations are so often herded by their ministers like sheep into pens, their only participation in the great religious drama limited to the odd hymn or an occasional 'amen'. For the rest of the time they are acquiescent, spoken at or down to, entertained or amused, and sometimes treated as if they weren't even there. After all, what is there left to say where religion takes its authority from unchallenged revelation?

Perhaps it is because religions depend upon revelation as a sign of truth that some religious people wait around hoping for something to happen, longing for a sign. If we wait for signs and indications our lives are left in suspension—dependent upon what happens next, things being right or going well, before we can be content with our religious lot. Our virtue and our happiness then lean heavily upon circumstance.

All this might explain why religions exist in an uneasy alliance with each other and why religious people who normally live in a state of quietism occasionally explode into raw aggression.

We can allow that revelation and tradition may be necessary for the time in which they break into human consciousness, but left by themselves within the confined space of formal religion they can so easily lead to inertia, even to the mindless acceptance of falsehood—as well as truth—and to the eventual stultification of our personalities.

It would be a radical revision of the way religious buildings were used if they ceased to be associated solely with the idea of a congregation being led and became instead a forum for questions, expression of doubts, discussion, learning, quietness and reflection. Fewer church services, mantras, rituals, and more spiritual exploration. But that would require a different type of priesthood and certainly a different sort of congregation from the ones that constitute the average church community of today.

The fact is faith has to be much more than a simple recitation of beliefs shared by other people. It isn't the acceptance of a set of texts or the assent to specific doctrines, or belief in a tradition. Nor is it a quality of waiting. Faith must be a living, personal experience, practised, worked out in our lives, through the darkness as well as light. It can be exercised by people who do not belong to a particular religious persuasion.

Faith is the underlying dynamic of human endeavour, the energy that links what is with what could be in all its glory and against all odds. It pushes back the boundaries of our limitations towards the infinite unknown. Faith is the measure of our true humanity.

Chapter 27

Truth Discovered

Only faith can substantiate.

George Steiner

Instead of depending upon revelation, tradition or authority the religious mind would do well to follow the example of poets and philosophers, that is to search for truth rather than wait for truth to be revealed. It may be that such a search ends up in silence, as George Steiner puts it:

> Wherever it reaches out towards the limits of expressive form, literature comes to the shore of silence. There is nothing mystical in this. Only the realization that the poet and philosopher, by investing language with utmost precision and illumination, are made aware, and make the reader aware, of other dimensions which cannot be circumscribed in words.

George Steiner, *Language and Silence*

What Steiner describes here in terms of literature we could transpose into a description of intellectual love. Intellectual love, which Spinoza so heartily embraced as the philosopher's ideal, is prepared to leave the familiar boundaries of institutional assurance and search the deeps for the truth that so easily eludes us. Let us say that this intellectual love is part of what we will call *pure religion.*

**Pure religion is the *search* for God.
It is an aim, not an achievement.**

Pure religion is most decidedly a journey into the unknown. It involves the mind, the body and the spirit. It takes leave of the tradition, authority, order, rule and regulation of religious structures and moves alone towards the infinite horizon of Being. Of course, it may be the case that revelation is part of that journey. For instance it is popularly held that the truth was revealed to Isaac Newton in an instant whilst sitting under an apple tree. But he didn't just sit there inspired by an apple falling on his head. He began to act upon that inspiration, or revelation, by investigating and formulating laws which had far reaching consequences for the development of science and human under-standing, proving that science itself is not static but a dynamic activity.

Why cannot religion be treated in the same way? Why does it have to be so fixed in its presumptions, mesmerised by revealed truth, overawed by tradition? Revelation should be a springboard to activity, to a belief in forward movement, a catalyst for spiritual experiment.

A journey into the unknown, advancing towards the truth rather than waiting for the truth to come to us, may seem too much of a risk for many, and especially for those who prefer the comfort of closed religious circles. But *pure* religion is an adventure of discovery. And for each one of us this adventure could well be portrayed as

103

an exploration throughout (and beyond?) the field of space-time—in the same way that creative and scientific minds explore the infinite depths of the universe around them. Once this premiss is accepted there is no limit to what the human spirit might achieve.

Chapter 28

Speak Up, not Dumb Down!

New opinions are always suspected, and usually opposed.

John Locke, *Essay on the Human Understanding*

Plato, Averroës, Dante, Leonardo da Vinci, Shakespeare, Isaac Newton, Einstein...the list of creative individuals is endless. Their task has always been the same—to present truths to humanity about science, art and life in whatever form is necessary to their purpose without sacrificing that purpose to popular acclaim. The effect is to lift humankind up to the heights of understanding.

But this approach doesn't go down too well in the modern world. The pursuit of excellence is now truly for the very courageous, for it invites ridicule and resistance from institutions whose members should know better. There are lots of high-minded people who in their fear of elitism treat heavenly thoughts with earthly suspicion. This down-draught of disapprobation is felt throughout academic institutions, in politics, the press, and in the Church, and achieves little—except, of course, to act as a brake on human endeavour. Genius is not welcome in a world of mediocrity. Where *are* the geniuses of today? They have been squeezed out by the clamorous world of mass culture and by those who prefer a life of ease.

This has great bearing on the problem of God. In the book of Genesis we read:

> So God created man in his own image, in the image of God he created him; male and female he created them.

> The Holy Bible (RSV), Genesis 1: 27

But what exactly was this image? I believe genius provides the clue. The creative nature of genius is the closest humankind can get to God. Without genius we are lost. We neglect it at our peril.

Genius represents true independence of mind. It is set apart from collective society, especially the one with which we are all familiar today. Beethoven didn't water down his music to make it accessible to the masses. He simply wrote what he had to write. Science would not have been served well if Einstein had diluted his Theory of Relativity. Mozart did not write too many notes but just the right quantity to convey his meaning.

'A calculated dumbing down is the worst: condescending and patronizing,' says Richard Dawkins.

> I worry that to promote science as all fun and larky and easy is to store up trouble for the future. Real science can be hard (well, challenging, to give it a more positive spin) but, like classical literature or playing the violin, worth the struggle.

> Richard Dawkins, *Unweaving the Rainbow*

We do no service to religion, either, if it is dumbed down simply to make it accessible to people who prefer not to think.

Perhaps modern religion should take to heart the example of the medievalists and revive the more scholarly attitudes of Islam and the Jewish and Christian Faiths during their enlightened periods. In other words we need not so much to go into the world to persuade as to retreat from the world and create centres of inspired learning where the spiritual teaching of ancient texts takes place without considering its usefulness or efficacy for a secular world. Only by a radical and independent revision of the basic tenets of religious faith will we come to a fuller appreciation of the remarkable opportunities that present themselves in these texts, not only to Christianity but to other religions and the wider world of human understanding.

There are always people who lead the way and pioneer the frontiers of human knowledge. These are the geniuses of humankind. We are now called upon to follow their example within the field of religion. The aim of pure religion is to inspire, to elevate the heart and mind into the infinities of heaven. To achieve this aim let us have the courage to look again at what passes for truth in religions today. This might mean disturbing the universe of our accepted assumptions. So it will not be easy. It will require stamina and courage. Revelation and tradition may have to be suspended as we search for truth in other ways.

Chapter 29

Finding the Right Key

*Sir, Pray be so kind as to let me know what you
esteem to be the chief qualification of a good poet.*

The Spectator, 1711-12

In our search for God we are actually looking for
a state of equilibrium. None of us finds it easy to
achieve a lasting balance between revelation and
a questioning mind, between tradition and a healthy
attitude to uncertainty, or between authority and the
exercise of personal faith. Once the overall balance is
acquired, however, it surely becomes the mark of
a spiritually mature person. Where then is the state of
equilibrium to be found? It is there in the classical idea
of art, where form and content, the logical and the
poetic, are combined.

The exactitude of logical definition and the scope of
poetic imagination do not easily align except in the
most fertile minds. But in the highest form of genius
they are found together, working from different angles,
approaching the subject from apparently opposite
points of view and finally producing the work in an act
of triumph. Nowhere is this more apparent than in the
field of music. And there is no finer exemplar than
Beethoven.

I am grateful here for a series of quotations in the book *Beethoven* by Marion Scott. In a reported conversation with the poet musician August Kanne, Beethoven refutes the claim that it doesn't matter whether a composition remains in the original key or is transposed.

> He defended his position on logical grounds, claiming that each key is associated with certain moods, and that no piece of music should be transposed.
>
> Marion M Scott, *Beethoven*

The precise demands of musical notation, the apparent momentum of form and the rules of composition together serve the poetic purpose—to produce music that endures and inspires. If either the logical or the poetic is sacrificed the object is lost.

> Here, more than anywhere else, do we get that curious feeling that in his greatest works Beethoven was 'possessed'—the mere human instrument through which a vast musical design realized itself in all its marvellous logic...We have the conviction that his mind did not proceed from the particular to the whole, but began, in some curious way, with the whole and then worked back to the particular...The long and painful search for the themes was simply an effort, not to find workable atoms out of which he could construct a musical edifice according to the conventions of symphonic form, but to reduce an already existing nebula, in which that edifice was implicit, to the atom, and then, by the orderly arrangement of these atoms, to make the implicit explicit.
>
> ibid., quoting from Ernest Newman's
> *The Unconscious Beethoven*

In other words, Beethoven was scientific in his approach to the poetic, which he saw as the highest calling of all. It is interesting to note Beethoven's view of inspiration and the relation between his music and religion. Scott quotes part of a letter about Beethoven from Bettina von Arnim to Goethe:

> He himself said: 'When I open my eyes I must sigh, for what I see is contrary to my religion, and I must despise the world which does not know that music is a higher revelation than all wisdom and philosophy...Music, verily, is the mediator between intellectual and sensuous life...Every real creation of art is independent, more powerful than the artist himself and returns to the divine through its manifestation. It is one with man only in this, that it bears testimony to the mediation of the divine in him.

ibid.

From these quotations it is only too clear that Beethoven understood, more perhaps than most, that the artist, poet, composer—and, yes, the scientist—all share in the divine art of creating something. But this creative act is a fusion of the intellect, or logic, and the poetic. Could this also be a description of pure religion?

Chapter 30

The Crystal and the Flame

> (of Leonardo da Vinci): *He had learned several*
> *languages, and was acquainted with the studies of*
> *history, philosophy, poetry and music.*
>
> *The Spectator*, 1712

Once we accept that the search for God extends beyond revelation and the traditions of formal religion, we will find there are further metaphors to help us along the way. The theme of the logical and poetic aspects of creativity has been captured eloquently by Italo Calvino.

> Among the scientific books into which I poke my nose in search of stimulus for the imagination, I recently happened to read that the models for the process of formation of living beings "are best visualized by the *crystal* on one side (invariance of specific structures) and the *flame* on the other (constancy of external forms in spite of relentless internal agitation)." I am quoting from Massimo Piattelli-Palmarini's introduction to the volume devoted to the debate between Jean Piaget and Noam Chomsky in 1975 at the Centre Royaumont (*Language and Learning*, 1980, p.6). The contrasting images of flame and crystal are used

to make visible the alternatives offered to biology, and from this pass on to theories of language and the ability to learn. For the moment I will leave aside the implications for the philosophy of science embodied in the positions stated by Piaget, who is for the principle of "order out of noise"—the flame—and Chomsky, who is for the "self-organising system," the crystal.

Italo Calvino, *Six Memos for the Next Millennium*

Calvino is fascinated by the juxtaposition of these two symbols. But the images are not limited to biology, language and learning. They can be applied to a vast number of aspects of our intellectual, spiritual and moral life and form the basis of aesthetics.

It is interesting how this theme is common to literature and music with little displacement of meaning.

Crystal and flame: two forms of perfect beauty that we cannot tear our eyes away from, two modes of growth in time, of expenditure of the matter surrounding them, two moral symbols, two absolutes, two categories for classifying facts and ideas, styles and feelings.

ibid.

Here then are metaphors for pure religion. The crystal represents the purity of doctrine, the formality of publicly formulated belief, personal discipline—the structure of things, logical reason. The flame is the unknown element of faith, the unquenchable nature of the spirit, the unpredictable nature of life, passion, and the majesty of power. The crystal is pure thought. The flame is experience. Neither must yield to the other. Both work in the harmony of opposites.

The need for system and the desire for freedom of spirit are component terms of pure religion and constitute in part the origins of the Scriptures themselves. It is no longer acceptable simply to take the Scriptures as given. Pure religion seeks to enter into the creative act that gave rise to the Scriptures in the first place, to identify with their origins, to be in touch with the energy source behind them.

The crystal and the flame represent the logical and poetic elements of the human mind. They are metaphors for the permanent and the changeable in whatever state of existence we care to consider. They suggest that even within the nature of God there is the possibility of the absolute and the contingent, the eternal and the temporal dwelling together.

Chapter 31

Many Dimensions

The mind remains unconquered.

Latin proverb

We humans are intended to echo the call of the universe itself—to create, to reformulate and to discover existence in all its varied forms. Our true well being resides in accepting our responsibility as creators. In our creativity we draw closer to the universe and to each other. And in this we are free, as free as whatever it is that calls into being the singularities and pluralities of existence. Sharing in creativity also draws us closer to the ideal of God, in whom, by definition, resides perfection of form and content. It would seem, then, that the concept of pure religion has as much to do with the idea of creative genius as with clusters of religious believers.

We find the deepest springs of creativity in art, science, philosophy and pure religion. These are, of course, different disciplines, yet they all require a particular attitude of mind associated with genius— namely the desire to understand. And this brings us to a point of relevance for pure religion. Quite recently there has been a considerable revival throughout these disciplines in their search for common ground. Art and science, for example, are seen to be more closely related than we thought. When we look at a Jackson Pollock painting and compare it with a photograph of fractals we can see a striking similarity between them. Pollock was painting in this manner long before scientists explored the mystery of fractals. It is often said that the music of Bach resembles a mathematical theorem, each with its own beauty and elegance. The construction of a bridge is more than a question of highly skilled structural engineering. It is also a matter of aesthetic necessity. The engineer and the artist have much in common.

Many books have been written which explore the links between different forms of knowledge and human expression. I am thinking of the lovely co-ordination of style and ideas in a work published by Flohic Editions that combines photographs of the sculptures of Alberto Giacometti and the written word of Tahar Ben Jelloun; the book *Poets on Painters: Essays on the Art of Painting by Twentieth-Century Poets*; Jacques Maritain's *Creative Intuition in Art and Poetry*; and the unusual work by Ernst Neizvestny *Space, Time, and Synthesis in Art.* Andrey Tarkovsky the filmmaker wrote *Sculpting in Time*, and recently a catalogue was published to accompany a series of exhibitions, concerts and events at Pasadena, California called *The Universe: A Convergence of Art, Music, and Science.*

All these works and many more go to show that there are cross currents emerging in a new renaissance where the barriers between the humanities and the sciences are once more beginning to break down. We are observing here the dawn of re-integration, the spirit of harmony, and a *religious* exploration of a wonderfully varied and elusive universe.

Chapter 32

In Search of the Infinite

*He that will enter into Paradise must have
a good key.*

Proverb

I n England some years ago, at a time of unrest and social and political uncertainty, one artist was conspicuous in his creative understanding of our search for truth. He was not afraid to call upon the insights of science, nor to accept that the scientist and the artist—and indeed the religious mind—share what can only be called the primary concepts of human knowledge. That man was Ben Nicholson. In the first of these two extracts he quotes a scientist who was probably amongst the first scientific writers to appeal to the popular imagination.

> I have been asked to answer a great many questions. I would like to quote the following from a speech made by Eddington, at Cambridge in 1931:
> 'Of the intrinsic nature of matter, for instance, Science knows nothing,...for all we know matter may itself may be mental.
> 'The old view therefore, that atoms or electrons are the ultimate reality, and that by interacting on one another in accordance with the laws of

Nature, they produce our minds, with all their hopes and aspirations, has no longer any scientific basis...Indeed, not only the laws of Nature, but space and time, and the material universe itself, are constructions of the human mind...To an altogether unexpected extent the universe we live in is the creation of our minds. The nature of it is outside Scientific investigation. If we are to know anything about that nature it must be through something like religious experience.'

Ben Nicholson, cited in
Maurice de Sausmarez (ed.), *Ben Nicholson*

Nicholson continues with his personal, artistic view:

As I see it, painting and religious experience are the same thing, and what we are all searching for is the understanding and realisation of infinity—an idea which is complete, with no beginning, no end, and therefore giving to all things for all time.

Certainly this idea is to be found in mind and equally certainly it can never be found in the human mind, for so-called human power is merely a fantastic affair which continues to destroy itself until it finally evaporates.

Painting and carving is one means of searching after this reality, and at this moment has reached what is so far its most profound point. During the last epoch a vital contribution has been made by Cézanne, Picasso, Braque, Brancusi, and more recently by Arp, Miró, Calder, Hepworth, and Giacometti. These artists have the quality of true vision which makes them a part of life itself.

ibid.

The search for the infinite, together with the integration of opposites, is becoming the new orthodoxy in science, art and religion. We now recognise the possibility that space-time is only one dimension of Being. Humanity stands at the frontiers of many more dimensions, hinted at, alluded to, in the works of artists, scientists and religious geniuses down the years. Religions themselves are being summoned by grace to attend the planning stage of the millennia of the future, for out of the chaos and lassitude of uncertainty new forms of religion are most certainly beginning to evolve. But it is pure religion that will provide the power of integration in our chaotic world.

Detecting directions, or even aims, may not be easy. After all, we were warned many years ago that whoever is born of the Spirit must be prepared for a randomness for which only the physics of the infinitesimally small can now serve as a metaphor of understanding. But the uncertainty principle in life can be accompanied by the thrill of expectation. We are guided by the rational *and* the poetic. Occasionally even the most scientific mind must yield to the dimensions of the unknown.

Chapter 33

Attempts at Revision

Change lays not her hand upon truth.

Algernon Charles Swinburne

Courageous attempts have been made to rescue belief from the straitjacket of sterile institutionalism. The suggestion was offered, for instance, that there is such a thing as *religionless* Christianity. The person behind this, Pastor Dietrich Bonhoeffer, put forward the idea that a Christian was someone who identified with the person of Christ, not someone who belonged to an institution.

Similarly, from within the Jewish Faith Martin Buber articulated a concept with which all of us are implicitly familiar. The theory is that there are two types of relation involving the I: the I–It and the I–Thou. This may sound simplistic but it strikes right at the heart of any system that treats human beings as mere cyphers. I–It is impersonal and treats the It as an object. I and Thou is a relation of personal quality and can never be reduced to the material plane.

> Through the Thou a person becomes I.
>
> Martin Buber, *I and Thou*

This is the essence of pure religion. As Buber indicates, the human being should never be allowed to be treated as an It.

Again from the Western tradition Rudolph Otto, the German theologian, considered religion to be the *mysterium tremendum* which human beings experience in the presence of the awesome force of nature. This is really a continuation of the *Sturm und Drang* philosophy that accompanied the Romantics, and is beautifully expressed by Wordsworth:

> And I have felt
> A presence that disturbs me with the joy
> Of elevated thoughts; a sense sublime
> Of something far more deeply interfused,
> Whose dwelling is the light of setting suns,
> And the round ocean, and the living air,
> And the blue sky, and in the mind of man,
> A motion and a spirit, that impels
> All thinking things, all objects of all thought,
> And rolls through all things.

> William Wordsworth, *Lines Written a Few Miles above Tintern Abbey*

Bonhoeffer, Buber and Otto all crossed the boundaries between the religions of humankind. They each in their own way prepared the ground for a fresh exploration of the nature and mystery of the universe and what possibly stands behind it. Their one outstanding contribution was to move away from accepted assumptions and make an attempt to redefine reality in terms of a purer, more refined religion. They were using a sense of the poetic to account for the depths of our experiences and beliefs.

Part Five

Think for Yourself!

Chapter 34

Protecting God

We may take Fancy for a companion, but must follow Reason as our guide.

Samuel Johnson

Reaching out to the infinite through art is only one aspect of the journey towards truth. If we are going to explore all the possibilities that exist in the human plane—especially the prospect of closing the gap between religion and science—we must also be prepared to think, and to think *logically*.

For many believers it is not always apparent why thinking is important in matters of faith, or to put it more abstractly, why reason is necessary to religion. What do rational matters such as philosophy and science have to do with God? Surely if God has been revealed through Scripture, and if the traditions of religion have become established by the faith of its followers, we do not need reason to intervene in the process? We simply have to trust. Reason cannot lead the soul to God. It cannot redeem, or save. That is how the argument has gone over many years. It is still heard in certain quarters in the Church. Reason is considered to be antithetical to faith, inimical to belief, and is often seen to be a cold and logical characteristic of the mind, whereas faith is an attitude of the heart.

The attempt by religion to divorce itself from rational principles and concentrate almost entirely upon revelation, tradition and authority on the one hand, and personal feelings on the other, has been disastrous with results that are only too plain to see.

The consequence of its surrender of the intellect is that religion today has little to say about the universe and human life. But things are beginning to change. It is now acknowledged that to deny reason access to the truth is the first step to denying the concept of truth itself. So if the aim of those who are opposed to the use of reason about God is to eliminate doubt, the opposite of that aim is achieved. They are not protecting God. They are in fact *exposing* God to doubt. For doubt arises not only from lack of belief but where there is an absence of evidence or inadequate thinking.

Nor does reason stand in place of our emotions in the search for God. To think it does is to miss the point of the search, which is to explore with all our available resources the infinities beyond and within us. Some of the greatest religious teachings bring this home in the expression of unity between heart, soul, mind and strength. There is no question here of feelings being closed down or suppressed where reason is deployed to frame our inmost experiences and thoughts about some of life's deepest issues. So too reason doesn't dispense with belief. We simply remind ourselves that the validity of religious truth cannot depend upon belief or emotion alone. And further, belief in God cannot stand beyond the reach of reason altogether. For if God's existence is not demonstrable to the mind in some way or other how does one arrive at the *knowledge* that God is the object of belief in the first place?

Chapter 35

The Contemplation of Truth

O God, the Truth.

Thomas à Kempis, *Of the Imitation of Christ*

Profundity and simplicity *are* compatible. And not all branches of religion seek to dispense with reason. The mind still plays a crucial role in theological debate and learning. Unfortunately, though, in the present climate there is a tendency to move away from genuine scholarship, bibliographical reference, lexicographical detail and heavily annotated works such as those produced during the medieval period of monasticism. Scholarly vicars seem few and far between. Extensive private libraries are seldom seen even in bishops' studies.

However, a change of direction is afoot. Some cathedral libraries like the excellent one at Wells are being opened up to specialist public use. It is a joy to see these facilities being made available to advance our knowledge of the early works of original thought. The immense richness of our Christian heritage—ignored for a considerable time by what can only be called the modernist mind—is now beginning to be appreciated once again.

What is fascinating, of course, is why this heritage came to be neglected in the first place. Perhaps here lies a further clue to religious decline—*trahison des clercs* in the intellectual field of religion, where the greatest error has been to divorce the mind from spirituality as if the two were incompatible. This error is now recognised by those in the highest authority.

In his Encyclical Letter *Faith and Reason*, published in 1998, Pope John Paul II urges all Christians to reconsider the role of reason in the life of faith. The two do not stand opposed to each other, he claims, but are in fact mutually necessary. In the introduction, for example, His Holiness writes:

> Faith and reason are like two wings on which the human spirit rises to the contemplation of truth

> Pope John Paul II, *Faith and Reason*

Later in the book, under the title 'The Interaction between Philosophy and Theology', Pope John Paul continues:

> As a reflective and scientific elaboration of the understanding of God's word in the light of faith, theology for its part must relate, in some of its procedures and in the performance of its specific tasks, to the philosophies which have been developed through the ages.

> ibid.

Philosophy (φιλοσοφια, philosophia) is reason in its most refined form and simply means 'love of wisdom'. Wisdom indicates a balance between reason and faith. So philosophy in this sense is *essential* to religion. For too long religion has tried to separate itself from philosophical nourishment and go it alone in the world of ideas. It is time to return.

Chapter 36

The Purpose of Philosophy

*All good moral philosophy...is but
a handmaid to religion.*

Francis Bacon, *Proficience and Advancement of
Learning*

Before we begin to reconstruct common religious truths—built upon the foundation of reason as well as faith so that the idea of God makes sense to the majority of people—we should invite philosophy into our planning stage. Philosophy has undergone considerable changes since Francis Bacon wrote *Advancement of Learning* some four hundred years ago. For it was around this time that Aristotelian philosophy, rediscovered by medieval theologians and incorporated into the beliefs of Christendom through succeeding centuries, began to give way to a new understanding of the human mind and the universe. This understanding has both harnessed the insights of the empirical sciences and provided them with their intellectual foundation.

But what has philosophy to offer in the debate about the future of religion? Even in its recent atheistic mode philosophy possesses tools of analysis which both science and religion by themselves lack. Without philosophy, science is simply a gathering of facts. In the case of religion, if philosophy is absent then belief in God is merely a collective dogma. But where will we find a useful working definition of philosophy to allow us to relate it to both science and religion?

In his book *Some Main Problems of Philosophy,* G E Moore described its purpose:

> To give a general description of the whole Universe.

If Moore's description is correct then philosophy, religion and science are related as siblings, for each discipline is rightly concerned about the nature of the universe. Philosophy can never really escape its duty to explore and clarify concepts of the mind, the universe and reality—in other words the context in which the term 'God' can properly be understood. Philosophy explains how concepts work, how they relate to each other and how they connect with the criteria of meaning and truth. Ideally it sharpens our understanding, brings power to methods of thought and guards against falsehood. The Oxford thinker Isaiah Berlin wrote:

> The perennial task of philosophers is to examine whatever seems insusceptible to the methods of the sciences or everyday observation, for example, categories, concepts, models, ways of thinking or acting, and particularly ways in which they clash with one another, with a view to constructing other, less internally contradictory and (though this can never be fully attained) less pervertible metaphors, images, symbols and systems of categories.

> Isaiah Berlin, *The Power of Ideas*

128

It is clear that such aims can be considered to be vital to the whole pursuit of scientific knowledge. But it may not be overtly so when it comes to religion. Some people, as we have seen, feel that religion doesn't stand in need of such treatment. However, in the sense that religion in its fundamentalist and pseudo-liberal forms has actually atrophied, we may conclude that Berlin implicitly, and rightly, thinks it does.

> It is certainly a reasonable hypothesis that one of the principle causes of confusion, misery and fear is, whatever may be its psychological or social roots, blind adherence to outworn notions, pathological suspicion of any form of critical self-examination, frantic efforts to prevent any degree of rational analysis of what we live by and for.
>
> ibid.

This surely is reason enough for us to explore the use of philosophy in religious language and in the thought forms of faith. We may not be able to express profound truths and experiences in language that is adequate, but that does not excuse the misuse of language or the confusion of concepts—including the concept of 'God'—that so often arises when religious statements are made. In these dark days of terrorism, conflict and institutional weakness, where hedonism is often accompanied by the loss of integrity, where identity and purpose are lacking in so many people and even in nations, the intellect is certainly one way of dealing with any impostors of truth. The emotionalism associated with extremists in the camps of the world's religions must now be tempered with intellectual purity and a love of wisdom. That is the province of philosophy.

Chapter 37

The Origin of Ideas

Man is yet free, during his brief years, to examine, to criticize, to know, and in imagination to create.

Bertrand Russell, 'The Free Man's Worship'

Anyone who wishes to enter fully into a rational debate about religious truths should be wise enough to acknowledge that philosophy is a battleground of ideas. For example, religious, scientific and philosophical minds disagree about the nature of the universe and about God; they also find it difficult to agree about the nature of 'Man', the term being generic for male and female. And here we encounter some ironies and contradictions which are not entirely unrelated to the question of God. Bertrand Russell in the book quoted above writes not only for himself but for many people today when he expresses the view:

> That Man is the product of causes which had no prevision of the end they were achieving; that his origin, his growth, his hopes and fears, his loves and his beliefs, are but the outcome of accidental collocations of atoms.

> Bertrand Russell, 'The Free Man's Worship'

It is difficult to accept that someone with the towering intellect of Russell could attribute his genius to such random origins in this way. But there is purpose behind his remarks. Russell's statement seems deliberately to have been construed to eliminate God from the universe, since to suggest that our origins are accidental is to imply that there is no design, and no purpose, behind our existence. The need for God is then largely removed. But he doesn't quite succeed. For it is scientifically questionable whether the formulated powers of universal reason, which are based after all upon laws of exactitude, can originate in pure randomness at all. And even if they can, the subsequent rationale of the human mind must have its origins in a prime order of reason of some kind somewhere along the line of descent for there to be consistency in reason itself. The mind of reason may have been chaotic in the beginning, but it cannot be said to be chaotic all the way through.

As in Russell's case, the scientific, logical mind doesn't always get it right. Scientists may criticise religion but it is science that is in the dock here. Whatever our views about the process of natural selection, it cannot be a valid logical deduction that our human origins had no potential for the eventual powers of logical deduction that we now have. In attributing the idea of randomness to our origins the evolutionists and scientific philosophers are trying to have their cake and eat it. It may be that the universe came into being and evolved by accident but you cannot have an accidental process of reason to prove it.

In fact the arguments of Bertrand Russell and atheistic scientists about our origins are no more valid than those of the ancient religious thinkers. They all

131

evaluate common facts and draw their own conclusions from them. Indeed religion could provide an answer to the question of random origins if only scientists—and religious people—would drop their prejudices and allow for wider Scriptural interpretations than we are used to.

Chapter 38

Do Be Reasonable!

Reason leads us to faith.

John Rotheram, *An Essay on Faith, and its
Connection with Good Works*

Let me now explain why reason is absolutely crucial to religious exploration. We all accept that reason belongs to the domain of the intellect, and the intellect finds its purest form of expression in philosophical thought. Most scientists would agree that reason is the employment of rational principles. And an acceptable definition of 'rational' is *that in which meaning may be construed and truth obtained.* Before we can say whether or not someone's words are true, for example, we have to be able to say what those words actually mean. So reason is to do with language, laws of science and laws of thought. But there is a wider, more spiritual application. It includes human activity.

We are constantly searching for meaning in our lives whatever the cynics might claim. Meaning is closely related to significance and nobody goes through life without considering that some things are significant. When certain things happen we try to work out what is being said to us by life itself. Events of coincidence often have a meaning even though we may not see what this meaning or significance is at the time.

Reason also includes the idea of purpose. In this sense all events in the universe, of whatever kind, are capable of *some* sort of rational interpretation. There is purpose within the hydrogen atom, for example, if only *to be* a hydrogen atom. Scientists measuring the effects of the HERA electron-proton collider in Hamburg are doing so for a scientific purpose, or reason. In other words, behind everything in this vast universe there is, potentially, meaning and purpose which can be discerned by an enquiring mind. To accept this is the first step towards engaging in a *spiritual* interpretation of the universe.

When we say that religion is about the search for meaning in life, or the exploration of truth, or the discovery of purpose, we are using the same terms of reason as any logician or scientist would use. In fact the spiritual aims of pure religion are similar to the aims of science.

Reason leads towards understanding. And that is the province of both science and religion. But meaning, significance, purpose, truth are not vain abstractions. They are essential to our lives. At this point science and religion cannot possibly disagree. It is how they interpret the fact that leads to a parting of the ways. If religion could divest itself of some of its irrational doctrines, and if science in turn could allow that some Scriptural statements are capable of scientific interpretation, the lines of demarcation need not be so rigorously drawn.

Chapter 39

Just a Word?

Therefore the philosophers were glad when they found out that nous, intelligentia...was the cause of all.

Lancelot Andrewes, *Lectures preached in St Paul's Church*

Many people will be surprised to learn that it is actually a religious text that rescues us from scientific scepticism and suggests that there *was* capacity for reason at the beginning of the universe—a rational principle within the very first instant. It may even come as a surprise to the religiously curious to learn that the ultimate answer to the question about our rational origins resides within religion. It is there in the Christian Scriptures. Both scientific *and* religious doubts about the true place of reason are answered in the Gospel of St John.

In the beginning was the Word.

The Holy Bible, John 1: 1

These familiar words ring throughout Christendom as they are read at Church services in celebration of the birth of Christ. The translation from the original seems

135

fairly clear and is accepted by every Christian as the Gospel. But some time ago I was faced with another translation. It came like a breath of fresh air and changed my whole attitude to Christianity and its relations both to other religions and to science. If it is correct this new translation narrows the theoretical gap between science, mathematics and religion to something infinitesimally small. Let us see what it is.

In Greek the passage reads:

Εν αρχη ην ὁ λογος (en arche en ho logos)

Educated people at the time St John's Gospel was written would have had no difficulty in acknowledging the historical and philosophical background to these words.

The meaning of the word 'arche' is considerably wider than simply that of a point of origin in time. It principally has two sets of interpretations.

(i) *beginning, origin, cause*;
(ii) *the first place, power, dominion, command, rule.*

From 'arche' we get archetype and, similarly, architect. The word seems to suggest the primary order behind things as well as origination in time.

The meaning of 'logos' is equally interesting. Its origins are in Greek philosophy, around the 6th century BC, when the word was used to describe the expression of reason.

> *Logos* as 'word' is never the mere word as an assemblage of sounds...but the word as determined by a meaning and conveying a meaning...*Logos* as 'thought' is neither the faculty nor the process of thinking as such, but an articulate unit of thought, capable of

intelligible utterance, whether as a single word…
a phrase or sentence, or a prolonged discourse, or
even a book. Whether or not it is actually uttered
(or written) is a secondary matter, almost an
accident; in any case it is *logos*.

C H Dodd, *The Fourth Gospel*

Dodd penetrates further into the meaning of logos and
suggests a universal application of the concept.

Behind it lies the idea of that which is rationally
ordered, such as 'proportion' in mathematics or
what we call 'law' in nature. These are examples
of the same thing that we experience as articulate
thought or meaningful speech.

ibid.

Within the concept of logos there is the idea that
rational principles not only underlie the human mind
but are at the very heart of the fabric of the universe
itself. For some philosophers, logos was the *source* of
meaning and truth. It was the rational principle that
upheld all things in the universe. If we were to say that
the universe—with its mathematical laws and the laws
of matter—was rational then we would be expressing
the idea of logos.

It seems, then, that we have here a significant
extension of meaning in the opening words of St John's
Gospel. Instead of the notion of a beginning in time
only, 'arche' could mean 'behind everything', 'at the
root of all'. And in addition to translating 'ho logos' as
simply 'the word' we could quite legitimately—and
more accurately—introduce the concept of 'reason',
'rational principle'. Indeed it is so closely related to the
word 'logic' that such an interpretation cannot be
ignored.

A better and more aptly modern translation of John's words therefore would be:

behind everything there is a reason

with a meaning that embraces science, art and indeed all human thought and experience. Further, it is only through the logos that we are able to reach the right definition and understanding of *anything*, including God.

John's next phrase—*and the Word was with God*—could be translated as follows:

καɩ (kai)	= and
ό λογος (ho logos)	= reason
ην (en)	= was
προς (pros)	= *towards*
τον θεον (ton theon)	= God

or:

reason leads towards God.

The verse ends with *and the Word was God*.

καɩ (kai)	= and
θεος (theos)	= God
ην (en)	= was
ό λογος (ho logos)	= reason

God = the rational principle behind the universe.

The New Testament is scientifically correct. When St John put forward the idea that a rational principle stands behind the universe he was writing in complete accordance with the axiomatic basis of science. The beginning of the Gospel is simply an axiom. Without a rational foundation science would be unable to proceed, religion would be void.

Part Six

The Convergence of Science and Religion

The Convergence of
Science and Religion

Chapter 40

Call in Metaphysics

There are more things in heaven and earth,
 Horatio,
Than are dreamt of in your philosophy.

William Shakespeare, *Hamlet*, I.v.166

The idea that there is a rational foundation behind the universe suggests that reality is not exhausted by space-time. We find ourselves thinking about matters which cannot be measured or observed—why am I here?—what is the meaning or significance of this or that event?—do I have a soul?—what stands behind scientific laws?—is there a God?—in other words, about possible abstract truths that underlie our experience and concepts. When we ask questions such as these we are approaching what is called metaphysics.

'Metaphysics' is a word coined by Aristotle in his work *ta meta ta phusika*, meaning 'the works placed after the physics'. But we are dealing with more than a simple name. The substance of Aristotle's metaphysics concerns literally that aspect of reality which transcends physics, that is, stands beyond time and space. Metaphysics isn't a licence for fanciful speculation at all, but is a worthy subject that demands hard work.

The question that needs to be addressed by the major religions is simple. Is religion based on metaphysical foundations? Indeed can there *be* metaphysical foundations, and if so how are they reconcilable with science? Or is the power of reductionism to prevail? In a recent book the theologian Wolfhart Pannenberg points to the necessary relation that must exist between theology and metaphysics if theology is to make sense:

> More than anything else, theological discourse about God requires a relationship to metaphysical reflection if its claim to truth is to be valid.
>
> W Pannenberg, *Metaphysics and the Idea of God*

He welcomes the revival of interest amongst philosophers in the quest for metaphysics:

> Christian theology must therefore wish for and welcome the fact that philosophy should begin, once again, to take its great metaphysical tradition seriously as a task for contemporary thought.
>
> ibid.

Perhaps with Cupitt in mind, Pannenburg seems to suggest that it is the theologians who are now one step behind:

> Unfortunately, theologians today rarely concede this dependence upon metaphysics. Nevertheless, the dependence is only too clear: a theological doctrine of God that lacks metaphysics as its discussion partner falls into either a kerygmatic subjectivism or a thorough-going demythologization—and frequently into both at the same time!
>
> ibid.

What then is metaphysics? And what is this battle all about? Who in the end is right? Is it Don Cupitt and the Sea of Faith movement on the theological side, and the successors to A J Ayer and the logical positivists on the other, in their collective rejection of metaphysical enquiry and dismissal of God as an objective reality? Or is it Pannenberg and those philosophers who are struggling to relocate God in a non-space-time setting? We can decide for ourselves, but only by applying our minds to the deepest of questions and dealing with them on reason's own terms.

Chapter 41

Into Different Worlds

*...the frenzies of philosophy, and the madness of
metaphysics, fill the disordered brain.*

J G Zimmerman, *Solitude*

With all the possibilities before them, philosophers, scientists and theologians(!) have no right to limit human knowledge to space-time only—and especially to the present moment, the now. What, after all, is the magnitude of now? What is the nature of the reality in which mathematical formulae receive their meaning and truth-values? Where are those formulae? In the mind? In the world of space-time? And what is the nature of truth? Are all abstract terms really reducible to empirical structures? No, the plain fact is that there are many different forms of existence of which space-time is only one.

We have already been given a broad hint as to what metaphysics is—the study of what stands beyond physics. Is it possible to go on refining this definition into something more exact, something that relates to everyday life and experience, assists us in our exploration of the hinterland of physics, widens the prospects of what may exist beyond the horizon of the universe itself and finally leads us into the domain of the everlasting mystery of God?

Metaphysics is understood by philosophers to be the systematic study of reality. This begs the question, of course: what constitutes reality? The answer is *whatever is.* But this is incomplete. There is a state beyond whatever is and that is whatever is not. The idea of reality therefore must include Being and non-Being as whatever is and whatever is not respectively. We can go further and say that reality also includes whatever might be. Any event in the universe may or may not have been, may or may not occur.

> **Metaphysics is the philosophy of**
> **Being, non-Being and possibility.**

Being, whatever is, must include time and space. But it is not restricted to time and space. The relation between space-time and Being is a relation between subset and set. We are part of something far greater than ourselves, greater than the world we see.

Chapter 42

The Logical Thread

To think, and to work, is to live.

J G Zimmerman, *Solitude*

How does metaphysics translate into practicality? Each day we exist between Being and non-Being. We are confronted by the facts of empirical events and the possibilities that surround them. But possibilities do not exist in space-time. We therefore make choices based upon what is actual—what can be seen or experienced—and what is not describable in space-time terms. This is true whether we are speaking about the moment at hand or the rest of our lives.

We are living all the time in a state that includes both the physical and the metaphysical. Science tells us that energy is continually being converted into the power of events in the physical world. But at macro- and micro-cosmic levels strictly speaking we should say that energy in *metaphysical* reality is waiting to be transformed into different forms of existence.

It is said that knowledge is power, but there is also power in reason once we understand that reason itself is belief in the possible.

> **In pure religion reason is a state of mind that trusts in the thread of meaning and purpose that runs throughout existence.**

This is true even though at times the thread may not be apparent in the chaos and vulnerability of the moment. That thread in its widest possible sense is what we mean by the logos.

We can now see a direct connection between the logos and the philosophy of being. Logic indicates a structure—the crystal. Metaphysics embraces logic as the refinement of reason into a structure of thought in the mind. It has permanent form which can be utilised with mathematical exactitude. 'Existence' covers all aspects of existence, all forms of energy, as the context of our varied experiences, permanent and contingent, and extends beyond immediate space-time. It is the flame.

This connection enables us to arrive at a working definition:

> **Metaphysics is the philosophy of the logic of existence.**

Metaphysics is the only possible common foundation for science and religion. Thus the 'logic of existence' is not merely a theoretical expression. It indicates both an intellectual *and* a spiritual way of looking at something that can be experienced. It expresses the relation between our minds and reality.

So let us see if we can arrive at a structure which is both metaphysical and practical, a structure that enables us to live our lives more fully, in which we can discover the logic of our being and which eventually will be seen to coincide with the truths of God as displayed in the Scriptures.

Chapter 43

The Structure of Being

Who does nothing for others does nothing for himself.

Goethe

I think many of us would accept that we live in a universe. It might be argued that some of us don't live in reality! But the fact is that the structure, or form, of the universe, and even of non-space-time reality, is such that for every thing that exists there is something else which is not that thing. This is true of concepts, of ideas, of physical things, of mathematical terms and universals. It is a law. The human being is part of this law. The ego is not alone. Nor is it the centre of the universe.

For every person there is something or somebody else—the Other. This is the basis of pure religious understanding.

Pure religion is the discovery and practice of truths and laws that reside in the relation I–Other.

Most people know what we mean by the I. The Other is everything but the I. It stands outside each one of us and represents whatever is totally objective and independent of our own existence.

148

The I–Other relation has a permanent, logical, form. It is always there, whatever we do and wherever we are. But because of the nature of space and time it is also dynamic in content—everything is changing and becoming something else. Although it seems to be otherwise, the I, the self, is never the same from one moment to the next. Our identity is fluid and not static. Similarly the Other is never the still, static object we think it to be. So within the permanent structure of the relation there is the Becoming. That is to say, new things are always coming into being and things change within their being.

We exist in the Becoming of the I–Other relation through our commonality in terms of space-time. That is why we all seem to be swept along by the currents of time and the winds of circumstance. Here the Other is particularised into the finitude of space-time. It is measurable. The Other in this instance is the object of science.

We also exist in the I–Other relation through the vitality of our poetic imagination. Here the relation is general. The Other is then the background for the whole of our lives, the mysterious connection between events. As we stand looking at the sunset or the stars, reflecting on our lives and where they are going, the Other surrounds us as part of a general relation. We find it in memory and imagination, perception and reason.

The I–Other relation is a valid formula for all that exists. For each of us nothing can stand beyond it. It is reality. We will never exhaust our knowledge of the Other, for it stretches into the infinite. Also, there is nothing whatsoever that stipulates that it must be restricted to the space-time dimension.

The I–Other relation is the foundation of unity in the universe and in human thought and experience.

The I–Other relation indicates that nothing exists simply for itself. It is in fact the prime relation in which we experience the manifold variations of life, power and moral values. Within this structure laws operate as surely as the laws of gravity or the laws of mathematics. The terms of the I–Other relation lend themselves equally, therefore, to logical, scientific and religious enquiry.

Chapter 44

Primary Concepts of Life

*The concept of matter has undergone a great
number of changes in the history of human
thinking.*

Werner Heisenberg, *Physics and Philosophy*

Allknowledge and experience is based upon the
concept that something stands in relation to
something else. You are not on your own.
This is one of the greatest discoveries of childhood. In
adult life it is a constant reminder of our limitations and
mortality. It tempers our egocentricity.

The question is, though, what is the actual
significance of the relationship between each individual
I and the Other? We have said that laws operate
between them, but to say what these laws are is to enter
into uncharted territory. Can science this time come to
the aid of religion? I believe it can.

If we were to reduce the I–Other relation to its most
basic form we would have the relation:

$$i–not-i$$

Now this expresses the essence of Boolean logic. So
what? you may say. What on earth does some obscure
mathematics have to do with religion? Well, Boolean

logic is the foundation of electronics and computer science. Either something is or it isn't. This is expressed as '1' or '0'. Upon this simple structure an entire system of knowledge and communication is built, with meaning and truth values that form the basis of information technology.

Thus the most essential formula of religion has the same characteristics as that of the sciences. And it is right here that science, in its most distilled form, can provide a way forward in our understanding of the i–not-i relation as a potentially religious structure. Let us see how.

In the form of the relation i–not-i the universality of logical thought resides and receives its significance. For instance, the formula contains all the primary concepts of thought without which thought could not proceed. These include particularity, identity, negation, relation, differentiation, conjunction, disjunction. The structure of mathematics is entirely dependent upon these primary concepts. In their absence there can be no science. i–not-i is the permanent form in which the primary concepts and the laws of science operate.

But the primary concepts also apply to the frame of religious practice and experience. Every person, for example, is an individual. Our individuality is an encapsulation of the logical concept of particularity. Thus particularity is not simply the first primary concept of logic, it is also the first primary characteristic of every human being. Secondly, each person has an identity. By this identity a person is known and recognised. It is expressed in the obvious but significant formula $I = I$. Further, every person is identical only with themselves and not with anybody else. To the I, therefore, every other person is a not-I.

The I–not-I formula is expressed in terms of a relation. This relation is capable of having values attributed to it. For instance, the relation can consist of differentiation or conjunction. Thus we are all different from each other but we do share common characteristics. And so the list of primary concepts goes on. For a more thorough analysis and a fuller explanation see my book *Zero Infinity Becoming*.

I can imagine some people saying, but what has all this to do with God? The important point to note here is that the relation i–not-i is always part of something greater than either of its terms. That is to say, each term is a member of the greater whole. Similarly the formula I–Other indicates that I and Other are part of something greater than either term. This may be called *The Universe* in terms of space-time. It may be called *Reality* in non-space-time terms. But the simplest and least philosophically complicated thing to do is to call it *Life*.

You and everything else other than you—at any single moment and throughout your life—constitute the Universe, Reality or Life depending upon which framework you happen to choose. Sometimes it is appropriate to think of one framework only, sometimes all three.

The construction of a philosophical framework is essential to religion, ethics and spirituality, especially if they are to speak to the mind as well as to the heart. It is only within a well constructed philosophical framework that proper discussion can take place about the meaning of religious and scientific propositions. But, much more importantly, it is only within such a framework that we can discover the meaning of our lives. Meaning is found in relation.

Thus the structure of pure religion is expressed in the formula:

I + Other = the Universe, Reality or Life

We should remember that at any moment, even in the state of our mortality, nothing can exist beyond what is represented in the relation I–Other.   It is wise to consider this when we contemplate not only the universe but the reality of God.   We cannot have I and the Other *and* God.   And if we identify God with the Other, as some theologians have done, this implies that the person of God is limited by the boundary of the I.

Part Seven

A Religious Understanding of the Universe

Chapter 45

The I and the Universe

Innumerable systems rolled,
And countless spheres diffused
An ever-varying glory.

Percy Bysshe Shelley, *Queen Mab*

We are not isolated individuals with defined boundaries of personality that act like walls. We are not fenced in by our own being or powerless in the face of the past, present or future. We exist in our own I–Other relation.

The purpose of pure religion is to inspire people of all persuasions to explore meaning and truth in the I–Other relation.

Tolstoy reached his conclusions about religion in a simple definition that takes the universe as a template:

The essence of any religion lies solely in the answer to the question: why do I exist, and what is my relationship to the infinite universe that surrounds me?

Leo Tolstoy, *A Confession and Other Religious Writings*

It is interesting that the universe is not what we understand by the Other. For we are members of the universe, part of it, and we share many of its characteristics. It doesn't stand over and against us, outside us.

Since we are members of the universe, it follows that not only do we share some of its characteristics by virtue of the fact that we are included in the universe, but the universe by the same token must possess the characteristics that we own.

Chapter 46

The Conscious Universe

...thought,
Which is the measure of the universe.

Percy Bysshe Shelley, *Prometheus Unbound*

What *are* the chief characteristics of the relation I–Other that will allow us to engage in a religious interpretation of the universe and reality?

To a very large degree, the problems that exist between religion and science—about God, the nature of the universe and reality—are also found within the structure of the human person. Are we simply material creatures with purely physical functions and lives limited to mortal, measurable existence or is there something more?

We all agree that we are physical creatures set in the dimension of space-time. But we are also people who think—we have minds. Except in areas of deep philosophical speculation few of us have trouble understanding the distinction between body and mind. Philosophically, however, the relation between the body and states of awareness is the subject of endless debate. And there are profound implications for religion in the outcome of the debate. For if it can be shown that the mind is a figment of the imagination, religion won't even get off the ground. Note the irony!

So how can we express the difference between mind and body in simple scientific terms? This is where metaphysics comes in. We are looking here for characteristics of the person rather than for categories.

Some scientists have attempted to reduce the mind to its physical elements in the brain. For them the mind is nothing more than a construction of atoms, chemical compounds and electrical charges. But the fact that we are located in time and space does not mean that we are totally definable in these terms. Our consciousness is something else entirely.

When we think we are not conscious of electrical charges at work. When we see something we are not aware of the mechanics of perception. Our perceptions and thoughts are not *experienced* in this way. We are aware only of what we see. The eye does not see itself.

Common sense prescribes limits to the principle of reductionism simply because human beings do not live in terms of the infinitely large or the infinitesimally small. Neither is a suitable category for everyday life. We are smaller than the universe, and bigger than the atom. In cosmological terms we exist precisely midway between 10^{27}m and 10^{-27}m.

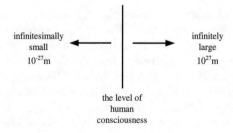

160

So, in spite of the many attempts since the philosopher Hume to describe the human being as a bundle of perceptions, we are beginning to grasp that we are not exhaustively describable in terms of bodily behaviour. Our person-hood consists of our states of consciousness as well. Consciousness directs our lives, and within variable degrees of freedom determines the co-ordinates of our being in the I–Other relation.

We are not always the victim of circumstance, as some determinists would have us believe. Our consciousness can be affected by the physical body and brain, of course. But then our minds affect our physical state. We are psychosomatic creatures. Our minds and bodies are interactive. The physical is only one aspect of our existence. And however many attempts are made to disprove it our minds are simply not reducible to the terms of space-time.

But a further important point arises here. Since we *are* conscious physical creatures, it is a logical deduction that consciousness exists within the universe. That is to say, there must be a framework of consciousness within a universe that includes the conscious I and the Other.

Eastern religions realised this many centuries ago in the concept of Brahman, the supreme absolute defined as the Divine Ground of existence.

> Our real self is a unique metaphysical reality, characterized by consciousness. According to Hindu understanding, the *Ātman* (the real immortal self of human beings) is the non-participating witness which is beyond body and thought. As absolute consciousness it is identical with Brahman, the Reality behind the appearance. Because the Ātman in the individual has total correspondence of identity with Universal

161

Brahman, its unique characteristics—eternal absolute being, absolute consciousness and absolute bliss—are identical with those of Brahman...In this formulation of identical Brahman and Ātman, two fundamental questions have converged: 'What is the universe?' and 'What am I?' Implied in this is an immanent Presence which is ever existent and is one.

Kenneth Verity, *Awareness Beyond Mind*

This is almost identical to the idea of the Ground of Being put forward by the theologian Paul Tillich just after the Second World War:

...the deepest ground of our being and of all being, the depth of life itself. The name of this infinite and inexhaustible depth and ground of all being is *God*.

Paul Tillich, *The Shaking of the Foundations*

We may give the name 'God' to the depth and ground of all being, but this doesn't mean God exists. It simply indicates that, if we choose, 'God' can be defined into the fabric of being by calling the depth of being 'God'—a somewhat circuitous argument which eventually will have to be unravelled.

Chapter 47

The Rational Universe

Ac theologie hath teened me ten score tymes;
The more I muse theron, the mystiloker it semeth,
And the deppere I devyne, the derker me thynketh it.

William Langland, *Piers the Plowman*

The universe and the human being are related by common characteristics. These characteristics are, if you like, gifts of the universe, and just as stellar dust bestows upon us the gift of material being, so we owe our idea of the principle of a rational universe to the outer reaches of the heavens. To explore this principle is the aim of science. Thus in the field of mathematics though new theories are continually being formed the principle of rational unity in the universe is always retained. Each section of mathematics is a microcosm of the whole. In science the various disciplines fit together like pieces in a jigsaw.

As we have seen, the ancient word for rational is 'logos' and this is the root of the word 'logic', the expression of rational understanding. Our logical and poetic search for truth is actually a reflection of the *abstract* nature of the universe. Conversely, the rational structure of the universe reflects the structure of thought.

163

This parallel nature between the mind and the universe is one of our most exciting discoveries. It suggests that the universe and our thoughts not only interact but actually influence each other. Indeed we can understand how Eddington reached his conclusion that the universe derives from thought. Also, in the great sea of consciousness it is quite easy to see how prayer is possible. Our minds and the beyond are very closely related indeed.

Chapter 48

Religious Experience

I see you have some religion in you.

William Shakespeare, *Cymbeline,* I.iv.153

It may be objected at this stage that our discussion
has led us away from God and has become too
theoretical, or too esoteric. But pure religion is
more than just theory and is certainly not esoteric.
Essentially it is grounded in thought *and* experience and
serves to unite experiences in the integrity of meaning
and significance. It is right here that Einstein declared
the purpose of science to be found.

> The object of all science, whether natural science
> or psychology, is to co-ordinate our experiences
> and to bring them into a logical system.
>
> Albert Einstein, *The Meaning of Relativity*

As in science, the concepts of religion must arise from
within, and be verified by, human experience. There
can be no valid conceptual system that does not take
our experiences into account. Tradition, revelation and
faith can be understood only in terms of experience. In
the case of religion it is simply that the logic is
extended to include the I–Other relation which without

experience, of course, remains an unproven system of concepts.

> The only justification for our concepts and system of concepts is that they serve to represent the complex of our experiences.
>
> ibid.

But we don't want to be too carried away with technicalities. There is room for these elsewhere. We just want to know whether our lives have meaning, and if so what this meaning is. We also have an innate desire to grasp the basis of truth in our lives and the world around us. I am talking here about the most ordinary level of our being where the simplest events require some interpretation and a level of justification.

With no meaning to our actions and our lives in general we are like wanderers in a desert without compass to give us direction. This is true of people in high powered jobs as well as those without work, mothers and fathers struggling to bring up a family, children at school—whether bright or not, refugees with no apparent hope, and those who are wondering where to spend their next share dividend. It is true for those who are bored with life and for those who fill every moment with activity. So this is a philosophical matter with considerable practical implications. And it can all be traced back to the primary concepts of life—experienced in the relation I–Other—which it is the duty of theologians and philosophers, scientists and everyone engaged in creative work to explore. Only through such exploration can we come to a wider understanding of the nature and meaning of our existence, to a deeper knowledge of the Scriptures, and to a fuller appreciation of the meaning of the term 'God'.

Part Eight

Engaging with the Scriptures

Chapter 49

To Translate or Mistranslate?

Translators, traitors.

Proverb

H aving established the importance of consciousness, and laid the foundations of a rational understanding of the universe and our place within it, we have shown that religion and science are closer together than was at first thought. But they are so only if we allow the barriers between particular religions to be broken down and common ground to be established between them and the claims of science.

Our next task is to explore the meanings of 'God' and 'Man' in some important translations of the Scriptures. We shall try to do so in a way that will take into account some of the important points discussed so far, and which will be acceptable to the modern mind of whatever persuasion. This is a tall order, of course, and no mean undertaking in the light of the rigid traditions of organised religion and the scepticism of science. But it is well worth a try.

We have to admit at the outset that though the different shades of meaning which these translations present are perfectly acceptable, they do take us away from the doctrinal position of much that passes for conventional religion. If we truly believe in the scope of fresh translation we should not draw back from a commitment to certain conclusions and inferences. And we must be prepared for some controversy!

When John Wycliffe translated the Bible from Latin into English the way was prepared for the reform movement in England and on the Continent. Wycliffe suffered personally for his endeavours. His writings were banned and his bones were later exhumed and burned. This act of ingratitude was repeated some years later when Tyndale completed and published his own translation of the New Testament in 1525-26. Almost all the copies of Tyndale's vigorous translation were traced and destroyed by his enemies and he was tried for heresy and put to death in 1536. It is remarkable how the Church rewards her servants.

Through the many difficulties that characterise only too well the circumstance of genius, both Wycliffe and Tyndale gave to the English language a richness and a poetic beauty that have endured up to the present and influenced the whole world in their turn of phrase and gifts of expression.

There have been numerous translations since those far off days, the greatest being the Authorised Version in 1611. In more recent times, however, the beautiful language of Chaucer's day and the Tudor cadences and subtleties of speech have been surrendered to more pragmatic purposes, the chief of which has been to be relevant. But in seeking to be relevant, recent Church-sponsored translators have actually sacrificed not only beauty for relevance but truth for ugliness, leaving the effect much worse than the cause they were trying so fruitlessly to pursue. It will be shown later that modern translators have lost a momentous opportunity for the Church truly to get to grips with some magnificent passages of original Scripture. By trying to follow Tyndale's intention to make the Scriptures more accessible to ordinary people they have in fact rendered them down to a level at which they not only fail to convey profound truths in a memorable way but succeed in convincing people that those truths are not worth bothering with. They have encouraged a light familiarity with the deepest mysteries. This is all too apparent in those circles where thought is not encouraged and banalities are propounded as important doctrines in the desire to equate religion with ease and pleasure.

Chapter 50

Truth, Reason and Scripture

*To say the truth, reason and love keep little
company together now-a-days.*

William Shakespeare, *A Midsummer-Night's
Dream,* III.i.150

The Scriptures contain certain identifiable truths,
which we call Scriptural Truths. But how can
we know that what appears in the Scriptures was
factually true in the first place? Our eighteenth century
clergyman put it well:

> There are four Ways whereby the Mind of
> Man can be rightly inform'd and convinced,
> concerning any former Matter of Fact. First, The
> Capacity and Ability of his Informers. Secondly,
> Their Credit with such Persons of their Times
> who were under no Prejudices. Thirdly, The
> Improbability that such Persons could be
> impos'd upon. Fourthly, The Folly and Danger
> of endeavouring so to impose upon them, if the
> Matter were not strictly true.
>
> David Collyer, *Collyer on the Bible*

What we think of as the truth may, of course, be seen to
be our interpretation of the truth. And it is interpretation

172

that affects the translation of Scripture. No single interpretation can be exalted to the state of exactitude, especially, as we shall see shortly, when we come to the concepts of God and Man. Instead of the hard-and-fast transmission of familiar concepts and the continuation of a one-sided tradition, new meanings can always be discerned and new truths revealed, hitherto undreamed of. That is the nature of Scripture.

So what criteria can be established for the correct translation of truths into different languages? They are not easy to enumerate but include the following:

(1) the original meaning should not be changed in the translation;

(2) the translation should be rendered into the highest quality language, which should be instantly recognisable as significant and memorable;

(3) the translated texts should themselves be an inspiration to religious, scientific and non-religious minds alike;

(4) the translated texts should serve to represent the original Scriptures in the spirit of the highest forms of creative genius;

(5) translation should take into account the philosophical concepts used by religion in its Scriptural and everyday discourse.

The original Hebrew and Greek texts of Scripture have passages of flashing brilliance which will appeal to the contemporary intellect if they are given the chance. The time has come for a radical retranslation, one that is daring and adventurous, one which will command the respect of the people once more as

173

translations have in the past. Whoever tackles this needn't be afraid of being labelled elitist. That didn't matter to the Hebrews and the Greeks, to Wycliffe and his successors.

Part Nine

Do We Need God?

Chapter 51

Exploring the Mystery

An honest God is the noblest work of man.

Robert G Ingersoll, *The Gods*

In the West it is widely acknowledged that relations between science and the Scriptures have always been somewhat tenuous to say the least, especially in the fields of astrophysics and evolution. Since the time of Charles Darwin those relations have tended to evaporate within the very first chapter of the book of Genesis.

Evolutionary scientists such as Francis Crick and Richard Dawkins dismiss the religious account of creation and its subsequent development with a sweep of the hand. In an interview on television chaired by Joan Bakewell, Crick said of the claims of religion that they were just plain silly. Richard Dawkins criticised the Church in the same programme for not exercising a curious mind about the universe. He felt religious people were too content to remain with mystery rather than work things out for themselves.

Some of Dawkins' colleagues would not quite agree here. Contentment with mystery *can* be an excuse for mental laziness. But the fact that science is rapidly advancing across many fields in our knowledge of the universe does not rule out its presence at all. In a recent book on modern astrophysics a footnote to the chapter 'The Early Universe' acknowledges:

> Whether the universe actually had a beginning in time and how time itself came into being are among the most compelling mysteries of cosmology.
>
> Bradley W Carroll & Dale A Ostlie,
> *An Introduction to Modern Astrophysics*

It is possible the mystery will be solved. But so far it seems that as the frontiers of knowledge expand and former mysteries are replaced with actual data and explanation, new ones emerge from the darkness of the beyond. Once this is no longer the case scientific exploration will have come to an end,

Chapter 52

Into Astrophysics

I do not manufacture hypotheses.

Sir Isaac Newton, *Principia Mathematica*

The Scriptures of the Church so often present a static world view which inevitably collides with the findings of scientific exploration and disagrees with the obvious by making an issue out of *non sequitors*. The New English Bible, for example, contains some elegant translations, especially in the Old Testament, but with certain important texts it often goes astray. For example it renders the first words of Genesis into:

> In the beginning of creation, when God made heaven and earth...

Now this sounds all right and would not normally cause the average believer to bat an eyelid. It is part of the doctrinal code of Christian and Jewish belief. But it is in fact a loose translation—and only serves to confirm what scientists see as a false argument.

The noun 'creation' does not appear in the original text. The suggestion that there *is* a creation implies the existence of a Creator, who of course is God, and that is why the text is translated in this way. But an assumption that has gone unchallenged for thousands of years is now challenged by modern science. The question posed by scientists in recent times has been: *is the universe a creation?* Thus Stephen Hawking writes:

> So long as the universe had a beginning, we could suppose it had a creator. But if the universe is really completely self-contained, having no boundary or edge, it would have neither beginning nor end: it would simply be. What place, then, for a creator?

Stephen Hawking, *A Brief History of Time*

Hawking's question is based on the conclusions of physicists regarding the origin of the universe in the Big Bang. The Big Bang represents a singularity. At the point of singularity the laws of physics break down, and the principle of cause and effect no longer operates. This can be portrayed very simply.

Let space-time be represented by a sphere. The sphere is bounded by its surface. If the volume of the sphere is represented by x, then everything beyond its surface is not-x.

In one sense we could say that wherever not-x and x meet is the *beginning* of the sphere. At one point there is no sphere, at another there is. That is how creation can be seen. The fascinating philosophical question here, as with the Big Bang theory, is whether a point can be determined where the sphere *both is and is*

not—giving rise to the Great Question: how did the universe begin?

But modern astrophysics is also represented by a different view of the sphere, this time the surface area.

Where do you begin? And in which direction do you go?

Where you begin a journey across the surface of a sphere is entirely arbitrary. There is no point at which the surface starts. There is no *before*. There is no *end*.

The surface, with no defined beginning or end, represents the singularity of the origin of space-time. The only laws that operate at the point of singularity of space-time are the laws of quantum physics, which in themselves embrace what is called Heisenberg's Uncertainty Principle. This means that at a microscopic level of matter there is randomness and an absence of regularity. Everything here is contingent. Events do not succeed one another as a sequence in time.

Does event$_1$ precede event$_2$ or follow it? In which direction is succession?

The laws of necessity do not operate at an infinitesimally small level—especially at the point of origin of the universe, which in itself represents a quantum dot without the co-ordinates of space-time existence. The universe cannot originate in time because time belongs, as it were, to the universe itself. What then does 'God' mean in the light of modern physics? What *is* creation?

181

Chapter 53

Religion or Evolution?

Human science is uncertain guess.

Matthew Prior, *Solomon*

Creationism—the belief that the opening verses of the Book of Genesis are *literally* true—is one of the great causes of disagreement between scientists and the religious mind. According to this belief the world (universe) was made in six days; on the seventh day God rested. Scientists hotly dispute this surmise and rightly so, for a simple reason.

The scientific mind has calculated that the universe came into being in an instant—at the Big Bang—and then took millions of years to evolve out of the primordial soup into what we recognise today as the universe of stars and galaxies. The evolutionary period was far longer than six days. But what is a day? It is the length of time it takes for the earth to rotate once on its axis. It is also understood as the interval of light between two nights. But both the earth and the sun are parts of the later universe. The time interval known as a day only came about because of the relation between the earth and the sun, and since neither was present at the inception of the universe, the universe cannot have been created within such a configuration of time—unless by 'day' the writers of the Scriptures meant something else.

Perhaps the religious construction of the universe needs to be revised. But whatever the Church's view, it has to be said that most astrophysicists and evolutionary scientists today see little need for God in their calculations about the origins of the universe. Religion, they claim, is not competent *per se* to deal with fields of enquiry whose subjects properly belong to the tried and proven methods of science—namely observation, hypothesis, experiment, analysis, calculation and proof. The Genesis account of creation is at best an inspired guess, and it is wrong at that.

It is all too easy to understand why religion and science part company at this point. But would those tenuous relations break down quite so easily if we appreciated more fully the meaning behind the mysterious words of the first book of the Bible, written three thousand years ago in the deserts and mountains of Israel? Would religion be so defensive and science so hostile if we dared to extend definitions beyond their current use? The prospect of bringing to an end the apparently irreconcilable issues that exist between science and religion, and even between religions themselves, is too exciting and too important to ignore.

183

Chapter 54

Genesis and the Question of God

Did God Cause the Big Bang?

Paul Davies, *The Mind of God*

What were the authors of Genesis trying to do? Many religious people will say they were describing how God created the universe. But no. Contrary to popular understanding and traditional religious belief, they were engaging the human mind not in squaring their observations of the natural order with the idea of God but, in terms of poetic and logical thought, creating an understanding of *the nature of existence*. The opening chapter of Genesis in the original Hebrew is a bold attempt to make a literary statement of scientific fact with a validity of intent quite equal to that of a modern cosmologist theorising about the origins of the universe in terms of the Big Bang.

The problem of the first chapter of Genesis is resolved by distinguishing between description and definition as we shall now see. The first verse of Genesis in the Authorised Version is not dissimilar to that of the New English Bible:

> In the beginning God created the heaven and the earth.

This is the familiar translation of the Hebrew text:

בראשית ברא אלהים את השמים ואת הארץ

(b'reshith bara Elohim eth ha shamayim veth ha aretz).

'B'reshith' means not 'in the beginning' but 'in beginning', in *any* beginning. It does not, therefore, refer specifically to the beginning of the universe. The root 'bara' certainly means 'to create' but it also denotes the concept of initiating something new. And it is further amplified by the expression 'bringing into being'.

So far we have *in beginning* and *brought into being*. The words 'ha shayamim' and 'ha aretz' mean, respectively, 'the heavens' and 'the earth'. But the interesting point here is the connecting word, 'Elohim', which we normally translate into 'God'. 'Elohim' derives from 'Eloah', God. But it also comes from אל (El) which means not only 'a god' but *might, strength, power*. 'Elohim' is the plural of 'El', and therefore could mean 'gods' in the conventional sense. But would this have been the aim of a monotheistic writer?

Or could it more easily, though controversially, stand for *the plurality,* or *totality, of power*?

For Elohim read Power∞ .

There is clearly great vested interest within the Jewish and Christian religions to protect the more obvious translation and idea of Elohim in its deified and particularised form. But the possibility of introducing an interpretation that leads away from the concept of a particular god, or even of *the* God, and which moves instead towards a reconciling position with science is not without appeal. This interpretation must not be dismissed simply because it stands eccentric to the traditional view. Indeed such an understanding of the word coincides with modern physics and any possible future physics that postulates the requirement of energy, simplicity and equilibrium to bring things into being. If power is realised energy then 'Elohim' (a word that first appeared three thousand or so years ago!) is not far removed from the astrophysicist's vocabulary.

Secondly, the words 'heaven' and 'earth' are in the order that agrees with a post-Copernican view of the universe. Genesis doesn't postulate a geocentric universe, as many interpreters have falsely claimed. It suggests a specific order of succession. But even here we could treat the words 'heaven' and 'earth' as symbols of something more scientifically structured than we have done in the past. 'Heaven' suggests an infinite stretch of the universe 'out there', while 'earth' implies finitude, limitation.

In beginning Power$^\infty$ brings into being the infinite and the finite.

To suggest this interpretation of Genesis is not to depart entirely from tradition. But it is to use the words as symbols for a meaning that extends beyond the familiar, and self-limiting, religious definition of God. Genesis 1:1 is more than an attempt to describe what actually happened at the beginning of the universe. It is a definition with which even the most ardent non-religious scientist can but agree.

The question for us here is: can we tune in to this power, this energy that exists throughout the universe? How do we direct our lives according to the energy within and around us? One way is in the exploration of

186

the i–not-i relation by the scientific mind through the laws and structures of mathematics and matter. But there is another, perfectly valid, way—that of poetry, art, music, sculpture. After all, why should the work of Albert Einstein, Stephen Hawking and Roger Penrose be nearer to the truth about the nature and origin of the universe than the poetry of Dante, the work of Michaelangelo, the paintings of Turner, or the Preludes of J S Bach?

Chapter 55

The Name of Power[∞]

...a Life beyond Life.

John Milton, *Areopagitica*

The story of Moses and the burning bush used to be familiar to every school child in the West. Not so now, perhaps. The story appears in Exodus, chapter 3. Moses lived in Egypt, where the Hebrews were enslaved. One day he was out in the hills tending sheep when he saw a bush catch fire. In the searing heat of Egypt, where temperatures can reach 110 or more degrees, it is not surprising to read of a bush catching fire spontaneously. Moses drew near and heard a voice. The voice seemed to be telling him to go back home and prepare to lead his people out of Egypt and into the Promised Land. This subsequently Moses did. But within the story there is a hidden agenda.

Moses was curious about who or what was speaking to him. Was it his own imagination? Was it an objective voice? It doesn't really matter. For what was revealed to the world at that moment was something of greater significance than the dramatic events that followed—greater even than the Ten Commandments, the Red Sea incident and the eventual inheritance of the

Promised Land—however important they may seem to Jews and Christians. Moses enquired:

> If I go to the Israelites and tell them that the God of their forefathers has sent me to them, and they ask me his name, what shall I say?
>
> *The Holy Bible (NEB),* Exodus 3: 13

The reply to Moses' question was quite simple and of few words. But it has posed a problem to all Hebrew and Christian scholars ever since. It is almost untranslatable. And it is this:

אהיה אשר אהיה (eyah asher eyah)

This is usually rendered into 'I am that I am'. The word 'eyah', I am, is closely related to the sacred name יהוה (Yahweh), which is translated into 'the Lord God', or 'Jehovah'. Religious people are quite happy to leave it at that, and have been for thousands of years. For them there is a God, the only true God, who rules over all. He is distinct from his creation. He is greater than all other gods. He is the God of Israel.

But to confine our understanding to this concept alone is a pity because it falls far short of possibilities. Behind it is a wealth of meaning that would answer many of our religious and scientific questions and help to solve once and for all a particular cause of doubt in our modern world.

The word 'Yahweh' is from the verb היה (haya) or הוה (hava) = to be, which implies existence, or life, without particular limit or predication. היה also means 'to become' or 'to come to pass'.

189

The Greeks in their own translation of Exodus 3:13 put it like this:

εγω ειμι ó ων (ego eimi ho on)

which means *I am Being*, or *I am that which is*. The word which we translate into 'God', therefore, means not *a* God but existence, life, being.

יהוה (Yahweh) = Infinite Life, or Life∞.

So there on that boiling hot day in the Egyptian hills it is quite possible that Moses heard not the voice of the Lord God, or the Lord of Life as we sometimes say, but Life itself, the sound of existence. You could, if you like, interpret this as the call of destiny, for that is surely what it was. You could also dismiss it as pure psychology. But it extends much wider than that. Here could be a revelation of the profoundest kind from within the very depths of the being of the universe. Moses was humankind in touch with Life∞.

So this is more than the story of some particular god hovering near a bush, although in its personified form that sort of interpretation is quite natural. It is more even than the imaginary voice of a man in the hills of the land of the Nile. This is one of those moments when, to put it in the words of Ian Ramsey, there is 'a cosmic disclosure'. Here the lines between objectivity and subjectivity break down.

Moses was not part of God. That, for conventional religions, would be tantamount to blasphemy. But he was, as we all are, part of life, of existence. What Moses did after the event was socially and politically significant for the whole of subsequent history. But what he is reported to have heard was infinitely more profound. It was revelatory of a truth that is accessible

190

to all, not just Jews or Christians but Hindus, Buddhists, Muslims and indeed non-believers.

The truth is that we can commune with Life, for 'Life' is what the word 'Yahweh' means whether religious people like it or not. And Life is the ultimate essence of the I–Other relation.

Chapter 56

Perfect Symmetry

*Holy, holy, holy, Lord God Almighty, which was,
and is, and is to come.*

The Holy Bible, Revelation 4: 8

We have discovered from the ancient Hebrew Scriptures that Life$^\infty$ and Power$^\infty$ are the terms from which the idea of God originates. The chief difficulty of our investigations, however—which we may not be able to accept, particularly if we belong to a religion ourselves—is that of symmetry.

If we define God as Life$^\infty$ this must mean not that Life$^\infty$ is a characteristic of God (therefore a predicate of God) but that Life$^\infty$ and God are interchangeable terms. Similarly with Power$^\infty$. This too must be interchangeable with the term 'God'.

But this raises a problem which is not too hard to detect. Surely if these terms are interchangeable with the common subject 'God' they must also be equivalent to each other? If they are, then Life$^\infty$ = Power$^\infty$ is true.

The answer is simple. First, God = Life$^\infty$ in the context where it is appropriate to speak of things in terms of Life. The same with Power. But there is another answer. It has to do with Absolutes.

Life$^\infty$ does not occur many times, only once, by definition. The only alternative to Life$^\infty$ is the absence of Life. Power$^\infty$, as the summation of all power, can only occur in one ultimate form, although it may have many instances. Thus when we take all Power to its infinite value we will find that we have Life$^\infty$. When Life is taken to its infinite value we have Power$^\infty$. Life$^\infty$ and Power$^\infty$ underlie everything that comes into being.

When we reach Life$^\infty$ or Power$^\infty$ we have reached what we may call 'God'. We do not, therefore, say 'God exists', for existence, life (חוה), is *part of the definition* of God. The formula is one of equivalence:

$$\textbf{God} \equiv \textbf{Life}^\infty \equiv \textbf{Power}^\infty.$$

The validity of this formula of symmetry derives directly from the axiomatic definitions provided by the Scriptures. If you find it difficult to think of God retranslate it in this way. It takes courage. In fact, strictly you can leave the word 'God' out and simply use the equivalent words.

But that would not be practical. 'God' is a simple term expressing vast complexity. From now on we shall write 'GOD', in capital letters, to represent our newly defined subject of pure religion, gaining a great deal and losing nothing.

Chapter 57

The Anatomy of GOD

For the Lord God omnipotent reigneth.

The Holy Bible, Revelation 19: 6

Once the definition GOD $\equiv$ Power$^\infty$ $\equiv$ Life$^\infty$ in their ultimate form of existence is accepted it is possible to consider this formula as the basis of universal religion. GOD is now seen not as a figure 'up there' watching over us, judging our every move, separated from the world, ready to reward good behaviour with gifts and meet bad behaviour with punishment—although the laws of the harvest still prevail: we reap what we sow. Nor is GOD to be identified with the psychology of our own make up, equated with our deepest feelings or profoundest thoughts. These images respectively are responsible for the fundamentalist position and the pseudo-liberal view. They are now obsolete and no longer required.

GOD is not simply the God of Israel any more. In this matter Israel has served its purpose. Nor, if Elohim/Yahweh $\equiv$ Allah, is GOD the God of the Muslims alone. Muslims, Israelis and Christians lose their territorial claims over GOD and their internecine arguments simply become futile. In the state of conflict that prevails between them their position is rather like

194

musicians in different parts of the world fighting each other over the truths of music instead of performing it.

Rather our understanding is that, in the term 'GOD', Power∞ and Life∞ (and Existence∞) are integrated. These concepts are universal. We do not ask, for example, where Power *is*, or if there is such a thing as power, or if power exists. We simply look for examples of power or decide that certain situations are what we call manifestations of power. Similarly we do not ask where Life is, or argue about whether or not there is such a thing as life, but consider instances of life all around us.

The big question of course is—who or what created Life? There is no need for this question to arise however once it is understood that Life∞ is not limited to the space-time equation and is not seen simply as an aspect of the universe. Rather, the universe is an aspect of Life∞. Once Life∞ is established as fact it becomes a fact forever. Like the surface of a sphere there is no beginning, no end, to Life∞. It is host to an infinite number of possibilities of which the infinite universe is only one.

To a great extent Life and Power are given. But the concepts of Life and Power are also inductively derived from experience and thought. They may contain insights provided by our understanding of Hebrew and Greek texts of Scripture, but they are not limited to these insights nor to the texts themselves.

Further, GOD is no longer a particular whose existence can be subject to dispute by science or any other discipline or order of opinion. 'GOD' is the term for a certain construction of absolutes, beyond which you cannot go. These absolutes cannot be restricted to a particular religion nor to the concept of a particular

God. You cannot prove Life, nor can you disprove it. Life is simply there, axiomatic to our own lives and existence.

Religions therefore are divested of their control of the term 'GOD' and everything that follows from it. Theology, the science or study of GOD, doesn't belong to the churches, or to religions, any more. It is on the list of everyone's potential interest. Doctrines of GOD and belief systems that owe their origin to an understanding of GOD have passed into the public domain. For GOD is now defined in such a way as to cease to be the God of the gaps in science in general and to be no longer the prerogative of religions in particular. Life, existence, power are not the possession of a particular religion, nor can they be limited in scope to scientific empiricism. They are experienced by all and are therefore accessible to all.

Chapter 58

Redefining Creation

God is the cause of all good things.

Clemens Alexandrinus, *Strom.* i 5

L et us allow that our interpretation of the texts considered so far is correct. Then the metaphysical boundaries between religions are immediately dissolved, as are the divisions between religion and science. Also a dynamic about our understanding of creation is introduced and must be dealt with.

This dynamic combines two distinct modes of thought associated respectively with the first chapter of Genesis in the Jewish Scriptures and the first chapter of St John's Gospel in the Christian New Testament. The poet Shelley distinguishes between them succinctly and appositely:

> Regarding those two classes of mental action which are called reason and imagination, the former may be considered as mind contemplating the relations borne by one thought to another, however produced, and the latter as mind acting upon those thoughts so as to colour them with its own light, and composing from them, as from elements, other thoughts, each containing within

itself the principle of its own integrity. The one is
τὸ ποιεῖν [to poiein], or the principle of synthesis,
and has for its object those forms which are
common to universal nature and existence itself;
the other is τὸ λογίζειν [to logizein], or principle
of analysis, and its action regards the relations of
things simply as relations; considering thoughts
not in their integral unity, but as the algebraical
representations which conduct to certain general
results.

Percy Bysshe Shelley, A Defense of Poetry

Shelley is getting at something very important here.
The Greek words he uses relate to two different aspects
of the human brain and correspond to two ways of
looking at the nature of the creative mind. They also
relate to the two different accounts of the origins of the
universe in the Hebrew and Christian Scriptures, and
reveal how the human mind can commune with GOD.

Some 270 years before Christ the Greeks translated
the Hebrew Scriptures into their own language. This
was commonly known as the Septuagint version, named
after the seventy or so translators who undertook the
task of translating the Law. In the Septuagint version of
Genesis 1:1 we find the word ποιειν (poiein) used to
describe the origin of the universe.

From 'poiein' we obtain the words 'poetry', 'poetic'.
The universe in this understanding therefore has its
origins in the *poetic* transformation of energy into
space-time, as a poet creates a poem. The whole of
Genesis chapter 1 is a description of the poetic form of
creation: 'And Elohim said *let there be…*'

Writing poetry is not everyone's cup of tea. But the
creative act, the production of a work of art out of
nothing, or at least from dissociated words, symbols or

the raw material of the world, is something we all do at some time or other. Creativity in itself is an exploration into the unknown. If you doubt this sit down and try to write on a blank sheet of paper a number of statements that express your thoughts and feelings. Then compose them into a cohesive whole. That is the essence of poiein and the beginning of poetry. Like all other arts, poetry is the combination of content and form and is a perfect example of the freedom of expression associated with both ברא (bara) and εγενετο (egeneto)— generation, the bringing into being of something that hitherto did not exist.

The significance of poiein, though, is not limited to writing poetry! It extends into the very depths of our lives. To a degree we create ourselves—what we are and what we do. We make our situations by the way we think and act.

By contrast, Shelley's λογίζειν (logizein) is closely related to the logos of St John in his account of the origin of the universe of space-time. 'Logizein' means calculation, analysis, rational account. It is through logizein that mathematics, astrophysics, physics &c account for the universe.

John's logical concept of creation differs from the poetic concepts of Genesis. According to John it is through reason that there is the egeneto, the becoming of the universe into existence. All things are here for a reason and through the activity of reason. This is not the same as saying that every event has a cause, of course, but even in a state of complex randomness rational principles are at work whether they are detected or not.

Quantum theory, as scientists will admit, is a combination of the poetic and the logical, contingency and necessity. It is also interesting to note that the ability to create and the capacity for reason are two of the major distinguishing characteristics of humankind. They are the foundation stones of a truly conscious civilisation, and possibly account for why we are here in the first place.

Part Ten

The Human Factor

Chapter 59

Adam, Eve and all that

Here are we, in a bright and breathing world:
Our origin, what matters it?

William Wordsworth, *The Excursion*

With the story of Adam and Eve we enter not the Garden of Eden but the lion's den. For here the controversy rages without sign of abatement. Never has so much energy been expended on something so contrived. There are futile arguments on both sides of the conceptual war. On the one side we have the progressive, scientifically orientated mind which rejects the Book of Genesis as an account of evolution. On the other the Bible Belt fundamentalists.

Notwithstanding, it is possible to consider the story of Adam and Eve from the point of view of truth, but only if we take the literal meanings of these Hebrew names and apply them as a general truth.

There are four Hebrew words for 'man' in the Old Testament: Enosh, Gever, Ish and Adam. 'Enosh' means a man in relation to large things—the tribe, the country. 'Gever' is a man in relation to very small things such as insects. 'Ish' is married man in contrast to 'ishah', married woman. But 'Adam' is not the name of a man. It is the name of humankind—man and woman.

The word אדם, Adam, could legitimately be translated as *man descended from the earth* (אדמה, adamah = red arable soil). It connotes humankind in its evolved state. This blows apart the notion that Adam was an individual person or that the word represents the male gender alone.

The book of Genesis gives an account of the origins of mankind in this way:

> [Life∞] formed man (אדם) of the dust of the ground (אדמה), and breathed into his nostrils the breath of life.

> *The Holy Bible*, Genesis 2: 7

Dust is the very point of origin at which science and the religious texts of Genesis coincide. We human beings owe our lives to the planet Earth. We also owe our being to the stars. For the constituents of our physical being actually derive from outer space. The remarkable thing is that out of the cosmic dust there was a vital component that caused carbon based life to evolve. From that carbon based life we developed the most mysterious and elusive aspect of our being—consciousness: the defining characteristic of the human soul. And this is precisely what Genesis is claiming.

How the view came about that humankind suddenly appeared on earth with no warning precedents, no hint of genetic development and no antecedents in the biological kingdom is beyond imagination. Why does the Church perpetuate such a view in the face of the scientific information available and, more surprisingly, with the meaning of the texts of Scripture so abundantly clear? There is no argument here with evolutionary Darwinism. No argument in fact with science at all.

Chapter 60

The Garden of Eden

Some flowerets of Eden ye still inherit.

Thomas Moore, *Paradise and the Peri*

To say that the Adam in Genesis is *literally* a single man walking in a garden is to rob the story of its essential poetic vitality and denude it of wider significance. Yes, a man called Adam could have been there and done that. Also GOD could have been walking in the garden at the same time, but only by altering the laws of reality.

In terms of the origins of humankind there is considerable common ground between Genesis and anthropology. The garden of Eden is identifiable as the land of Babylon between the Tigris and the Euphrates, now known as Iraq.

> And the LORD God planted a garden eastward in Eden; and there he put the man whom he had formed.
>
> *The Holy Bible*, Genesis 2: 8

> And the fourth river is Euphrates.
>
> ibid. 2: 14

Anthropologists suggest that civilisation as we know it today was born in the area of Iraq. Here the ideas of language, numeracy, laws, were founded. The area is a focus for history, religion, war and reconciliation. Abraham, the Patriarch from whom descend the religions of the Jews, Christians and Muslims, began his career in Ur of the Chaldees to the south of Babylonia, the land of Sumer and Akkad. The Sumerians gave us literature, religion, artefacts for everyday life and forms of institutions which are still in use today. This is perhaps where the rational consciousness of the West was born.

If the origins of civilisation are to be found here it is all the more important for us to recognise the significance of those texts which refer to this region—if only from the point of view of our human continuity and survival. Once again the poetic insights of the human mind capture truths that can so easily elude scientific investigation. The geographical location of Genesis is probably scientifically accurate even though it is an ancient text, poetically written and lacking the credibility of statistical analysis.

Chapter 61

Mother Nature

> Nature abhors a vacuum.
>
> Latin Proverb

With the sheer force of translation we are compelled to understand Adam as the signification of humankind. But what of Eve and the Fall, that most ubiquitous of stories?

If Adam was not a particular man, except for a characterisation part in a wonderful story, who was Eve? Again we are called upon to exercise our imagination and extend beyond the boundaries of rigidity that have existed for so long through the traditions and translations of the Church. After all, how could Eve be a particular woman if Adam means humankind—including, that is, men *and* women? The fact is, she isn't.

In the story of Genesis the word 'Eve' appears for the first time in chapter 3 verse 20:

> And Adam called his wife's name Eve

'Well, there you are,' says the literalist, 'Eve is the wife of Adam. Your hypothesis falls at this point. Humankind cannot have a wife.' No, but metaphorically humankind *can* be married—to ideas, to customs, to habits, to the world.

Let us look at the word 'Eve' more closely. In Hebrew it is a proper name, חוה (Khav-vah) and in appearance is virtually a carbon copy of the name Yahweh. Now 'Yahweh', as we know, is constructed from the word חוה (hava) which means 'life'. And lo and behold, 'Khav-vah' also signifies life.

Eve = life-giver.

There is no word in Hebrew for 'nature'. Could it be possible, therefore, that by the word 'Eve' the author meant life-giving nature, *Mother* Nature?

Eve = Mother Nature.

If this is so then it is not too hard to see how Adam, Eve, and GOD are related analogically at different levels of interpretation:

The Story	Adam	- a man
	Eve	- his wife
	Yahweh	- the Lord
The Analogy	Adam	- Humankind
	Eve	- Nature
	Yahweh	- Life

Each account takes place within the I–Other relation, but it is the analogical reference rather than the story that lends itself to literal truth.

Chapter 62

The Fall

*From the Fall it is but a short step in man's
history to the Flood.*

John Davison, *Discourses on Prophecy*

The story of Adam and Eve depicts the Fall of
Man. But this fall is set against the backdrop of
the opening verses of Genesis. In beginning
Power∞ (GOD) brought into being the infinite heavens
and the finite earth. The name of this power is Life∞
(LORD GOD). There is humankind (Adam) and nature
(Eve).

'The Fall' is a descriptive noun used to indicate
the turning away of humankind from Life∞ and, by
deliberation, limiting the psyche to the boundaries of
our nature in space-time. The Fall, therefore, represents
the substitution of one dimension for another—nature
for GOD, the finite for the infinite. That is, חוה for יהוה.

In reality humankind is constantly faced with
a power struggle—the choice between a life of power
and the power of life. We are confronted by the
possibility of opposites. The truth of this possibility
belongs to the universe and humankind. It does not
belong to a particular religion, whatever that religion
might be. Rather, we grasp its significance as the basis

for a general understanding about the nature and experience of human will. It is our conscious, human will that directs what we shall be. Human integrity is built on the choices we make.

The Fall brilliantly portrays the condition of human nature where we choose to limit our horizons by narrow mindedness, reduce our vision or hope, and confine our interests to the immediate moment in space-time. In so doing we sacrifice the vast potential that exists in our lives.

Part Eleven

Living Life to the Full

Chapter 63

The Direction of Life

What's past is prologue.

William Shakespeare, *The Tempest*, II.i.261

In our examination of the ancient Hebrew Scriptures we have arrived at some astounding yet valid conclusions about GOD and humankind. Can the New Testament provide us with similar surprises?

The Christian Gospel begins with three familiar concepts relating to the Fall: sin, repentance and forgiveness. In St Mark, chapter 1 verse 4, John the Baptist appears in the wilderness proclaiming:

βαπτισμα μετανοιας εις αφεσιν αμαρτιων
(baptisma metanoias eis aphesin hamartion)

This is traditionally translated into 'a baptism of repentance for the forgiveness of sins'. But why do these words fall on deaf ears today? Because this and like verses in the New Testament have too limited a view to speak to the rising generation or to cross the reservations and boundaries of religious belief. The Gospel itself needs to be liberated from the concepts of constraint. So let us now translate this passage into something we can understand in terms of modern life.

We all want to enrich our existence, to reach out to the prospects that life has to offer in the I–Other relation. For some this is an exceedingly restricted operation. Poverty, illness and loss tend to narrow our boundaries. Religion teaches that the purpose of life partly consists in accepting circumstance. Acceptance *can* be a powerful response, but it is not the whole answer. The prescription for human success is to understand the laws of life.

Everything is governed by law, even at a microcosmic level. Possibility itself is a question of law. Without law there would be no statistics of probability. It is against the background of law in the universe that we are able to direct our lives.

Imagine your life as a circle. The circumference represents your limit. You can point away from everything outside that circle and inwards to the centre of your self. If we think of our lives as being part of Life$^\infty$ then within our own space-time continuum we can aim towards Life$^\infty$ or away from it. We can expand the boundaries of our existence or narrow them.

To aim away from the infinite possibilities of Life could be considered to be 'aiming in the wrong direction'. This is a phrase that is expressed by the Greek word ἁμαρτια (hamartia).

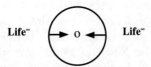

In the Christian Scriptures 'hamartia' is usually translated into the word 'sin'. But this gives it a moral connotation which is misleading. Rather—and more fully—it means *to miss the mark*, *fall short*, or *fail in*

214

one's purpose. 'Hamartia' is an expression that can be applied to every aspect of life where human beings fail to realise their potential. You can aim a yacht towards the rocks; that is hamartia. You can become depressed; that too is hamartia. An accident, a natural tragedy, ignoring your destiny, not enjoying work, illness, boredom—all these are indicative of the same concept. There *is* a moral content to this concept, but the concept is not restricted to a moral or ethical dimension. It indicates, rather, a state of being.

> **In the context of Life[∞] hamartia indicates a failure, either by act of will *or* through circumstance, to fulfill one's purpose to live life abundantly or possess life abundantly.**

The translation of the word 'hamartia' into 'sin' is too narrow to speak to the human condition today. For sin has the connotation of *doing* wrong—in other words sin is something that is our own fault and for which we will be punished by exclusion from God unless we seek his forgiveness.

It is often thought that the duty of religions is to bring human beings back on course by pointing out that they are sinners. This itself now needs correcting. It cannot be within the compass of a tightly restricted religion to preach to others the philosophy behind hamartia. For unless the religion sees within itself the object lesson of its own message the words 'Physician, heal thyself' (Luke 4:23) will get in the way of that message to the world. Because they have frequently, indeed consistently, ignored the possibilities of pure religion, religions themselves could be said to have been aiming in the wrong direction for many years. Their arguments, their wars, their pettiness, their failure to inspire the noblest deeds, their obsession with self-promotion and institutional survival suggest that religions stand in need of redemption as much as the world does. It is easy to see how this fact eludes religions if they see themselves as entirely on the side of God, dispensing forgiveness to those who are defined as sinners.

Hamartia *embraces* religion. It may be necessary to resist the pull of religion altogether if it is pointing in the wrong direction. Does the human soul require institutional religion if it is to point itself in the direction of Life∞? Can it not do this unaided? Yes, indeed it can.

Chapter 64

Getting Back on Course

Lord! we know what we are, but know not what we may be.

William Shakespeare, *Hamlet*, IV.v.43

Ｔhe ultimate purpose of pure religion is to inspire people to aim towards the richness of Life∞ in whatever sphere they find themselves. If any religion fails to achieve this—by, for example, condemning people who fall away from the ideal—it quite simply fails to be a true religion. Scriptures, buildings, priests all fall short if the ideal of pointing people in the direction of Life∞ is not attained.

As we have just seen, one's life is like a circle set within the Infinite. One can point inwards, to zero, or travel round the circumference. Both are a weariness to the soul. The procedure, if that is the right word, for someone to follow in order to turn away from the condition of hamartia and towards Life∞ is quite simple. It involves changing direction through an act of faith and will.

This is what is meant in the Christian New Testament by μετανοια (metanoia). 'Metanoia' consists of two parts: *meta*, change, and *noia,* mind, or purpose. It is to set the mind in the right direction. From the Christian Scriptures it is translated into the word 'repentance'. But metanoia, strictly, does not mean to be sorry for what you have done. That is in a sense the passive voice. It is, rather, to be active, to do something positive—the description of intention, not the inert admission of culpability.

Metanoia refers to any condition in which the human being develops the inner criterion of discernment between perfection and imperfection, between what is possible and what is actual. The artist, for example, struggles for truth within this tension of opposites. The writer, too, with attentive concern for exactitude of expression, strives within this plane. The mother has an instinctive desire to nourish her child and equip that child for the future. The craftsman aims towards perfection. The ideal may never be achieved. But it would be a sorry world without this notion of direction.

The teaching of metanoia applies to individuals, institutions and the state. It is possible for a whole nation to change its direction. But it is more aptly used of individuals who re-energise their lives by aligning with the principles of life, power and reason.

In pure religion metanoia is to change direction away from the zero or circuitousness of being and towards the Infinite.

This new understanding of repentance liberates us from the injunctions of formalised religion and introduces the freedom of personal responsibility. Indeed, formality cannot speak to the heart and mind about repentance except through the discipline of conscience. There, deep within the human consciousness where conscience operates, the imperative of what is right can come into being—the word, again, is εγενετο (egeneto), the dynamic of becoming—only by the conversion of intent. Religion cannot enforce repentance.

To change the direction of the mind is to exercise an act of will in response to the call of grace. Grace is given for our benefit from beyond the circle of our being. It is charged with the fullness of Being and the infinite possibility of Life.

Consider those thoughts, feelings, attitudes and events that pull you down, or back. Translate them into something positive. That is what pure religion is about—transcending one's circumstances and getting back on course.

Chapter 65

Life Style

The will to do, the soul to dare.

Sir Walter Scott, *The Lady of the Lake*

We long to extend beyond the limitations that exist in our lives, to be masters of our own destiny, to escape from the grip of uncertainty and the misunderstandings that occur all around us. We yearn for a lasting freedom from the confinements of dull routine and everyday necessity and long for that sense of liberation that will allow us, at last, to be ourselves, to set our souls free from the restrictions and continuing reminders of mortality. But we cannot flee from the truth.

> **Only by aiming in the right direction
> can we experience freedom of spirit.**

The cry of the secular heart in the West is for personal fulfilment. In this cry, though, there is also a lament—a lament for the enigmatic loss of innocence, for the absence of deep and abiding contentment with our lot and for the general lack of continuity of hope. In the secular age, freedom is duplicitous. Simplicity of soul has been surrendered to the complexity of system. Being is poised on the edge of non-Being. Our contingency, marked by frustration and doubt, is no longer cause for rejoicing. It could be said that in the West we are suffocating under the burden of change. Variety, of course, is still the elusive goal in our intensive and endless search for that something else in relationships, but it is no longer equated with the spice of life. It has become the template of boredom. We are satiated with unquantifiable abundance and our future is thereby diminished.

The human condition now is to surrender to ever increasing change of job, of partner, of personal image—that is the direct consequence of pseudo-liberalism. Often pseudo-liberalism is a reaction against moral compulsion, whereas false religion is guided by fear of defection. Both are equally insincere. Pure religion, on the other hand, teaches a new way. Inspired by hope it points us towards the Infinity of Being rather than towards the zero of our own being.

To set our minds on things that are 'above' in the scale of human values we are called upon to let go—of the self and of our control of others and indeed the domination of ourselves by others—and point our lives in the direction of boundless possibility. This is difficult, but it can be done. Metanoia. In achieving this we discover liberty and the laws of life.

Chapter 66

Release

Who then is the helmsman of necessity?

Aeschylus, *Prometheus Bound*

Just as we wish to be set free from certain circumstances at hand, so we also reach out for things that are distant and hope for states of possibility. The two matters are not entirely separable. The psychological, empirical and spiritual consequence of metanoia is αφεσις (aphesis), another Greek word that appears throughout the Christian New Testament. 'Aphesis' is normally translated into 'forgiveness'. Its richer and broader meaning however is 'release'. And that makes the whole dynamic of hamartia, metanoia and aphesis of much wider appeal than the tired old formula, however formally correct, of sin, repentance and forgiveness, related as it has been for hundreds of years with the power of the Church.

> **Release from the gravitational pull of the here and now of mortality and the finitude with which we are all familiar introduces a lightness of being. Release is the necessary condition of transcendence.**

Many of us are trapped in the bonds of being. We are unable to let go, to enter into the fulless of life—

restricted by inhibition, illness, fear of judgement and ultimate failure. And much of this is related to our false image of God.

To be released is to be set free from false images and negative attitudes into the infinite prospects of the I–Other relation.

Above all it should be the purpose of religion to enable this to happen. But religion cannot be considered to be the instrument of aphesis unless it, too, experiences release. For the mechanical formulae of dogma and ritual serve only to entrap religion in the bonds of servitude. Its priests and other functionaries merely perform the rites and ceremonies of dead habit. The meaning has been lost. Unless, that is, and until, the great change is brought about. The stasis of religion itself stands in need of release. Let it come.

Part Twelve

Practical Spirituality

Chapter 67

Towards Spirituality

In spirit and in truth.

The Holy Bible, John 4: 24

It is time to draw together the various strands of our investigation. We have accepted the need to restore religious truth to its metaphysical foundations. We have also discovered insights from key concepts in the original languages of the Holy Scriptures. Both aspects of our brief survey provide us with material for a new understanding of old and familiar truths about GOD and Man. We can now consolidate our position and reach towards a concept of universal religion based upon what we have found. This means formulating a new spirituality for the age—providing a foundation for our future understanding of the universe around us and the nature of human life.

In one sense religion and science are exact opposites in their treatment of the human being. Although science seeks to establish general principles behind physical phenomena it is, as we have seen, mainly reductionist in its approach to human behaviour and wary of matters that are not configurable in empirical or mathematical terms. Pure religion on the other hand seeks to establish a domain that transcends the physical.

But that doesn't mean it is removed from everyday experience.

In our conscious minds we are aware of our physical being. But we are also conscious of something else in our nature, something that extends beyond our thoughts, perceptions, emotions and physical states. This is to do with who and what we *are*. It is spiritual.

> **The spiritual is that which transcends the material and intellectual planes of being.**

The Hebrew word for 'spirit' is רוח (ruach); the Greek is πνευμα (pneuma). Both also mean 'breath', 'wind', hence 'the breath of life'. Breath is air, space. Without it life collapses. So 'spirit' is associated with the notion of inspiration. It is like breath to our being—the energising power of our lives. To lose the spirit is in effect to exist in a state of expiration.

As breath is associated with health, so the spiritual life is closely connected with a sense of well-being. Both are related to wholeness. In each case our well-being depends on the relations we have with our environment.

> **We are related spiritually to the infinite Other. This relation defines who and what we are. It is inexhaustible.**

228

Chapter 68

The Soul

...and with thy soul of flame.

Samuel Rogers, *Italy*

The soul is de rigueur.

Samuel Beckett, *How It Is*

Taken together the dimensions of the intellectual, the material and the spiritual in a person constitute what we mean by 'the soul'. Once widely accepted in thinking circles, the concept of soul ceased to be respectable when philosophy took a turn for the worse and deselected metaphysics from its vocabulary. The term was quickly taken up by the new science, psychology, which then ironically rejected the idea of the soul even though the word 'psychology' was quarried in the first place from the Greek ψυχη (psuché) which means, er, 'soul'.

This has happened before. 'Biology' once meant the study of human life (Greek: βιος, bios). It is as though once science has adopted a term it squeezes out the original meaning then uses the newly defined parameters to disprove its origins. This is not always justified. After all 'science' itself simply means 'knowledge'. As such it has no rights of limitation except in the adoption of method.

Is there a science of the soul that extends beyond the empirical subtleties of psychology? Is there a personology, that treats *the person* as a suitable object of study? And does the study of the person always have to result in the reduced circumstances of analytic science?

The soul is to be understood not simply as an intellectual category but as the complex of different forms of being. Using the symbol of the circle, it is clear from our discussion so far that we can point our lives in three directions: inwards, around, or outwards.

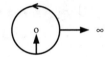

But the circle may also be transformed into a cone. As we point in the direction of Infinity, beyond the limit of our own being, so we move deeper into Being itself.

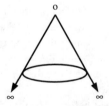

Every person lives in three main planes of being—the physical plane of space-time, the mental plane of mind and the plane of the spiritual.

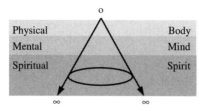

Each plane of being is located in its own definable space. We have, for example, physical space which is the measure of our freedom to exist in terms of space-time. We have intellectual space, the measure of our freedom to think, and spiritual space which is the measure of our capacity to be who we are. We have no right to trespass on the space of others in any or all of the three planes.

When the planes of one's being are combined into a whole, we have the identity of the soul. The soul is not exhaustively definable by any one plane but consists of all three.

Each soul exists in its own rational space.

Rational space is where meaning, truth and purpose can be discerned and formulated and is necessary to both science and pure religion. Rational space is the most fundamental aspect of our conscious existence. It is the foundation of knowledge, understanding and spirituality. We have the right to protect our rational space. It is within such space that we discover who we are.

231

Chapter 69

The Depth of Being

Would I were assur'd of my condition!

William Shakespeare, *King Lear*, IV.vii.56

T he soul is the receptor and distributor of power within different planes of being. In each plane we can experience the realisation of the energy of life, or we can experience its blockage or misdirection, resulting in entropy and a loss of equilibrium. It's up to us. If the following diagram represents a person's soul then the spirituality of that person can be measured in two ways: by the depth of the line o→∞ and by the width of the angle α.

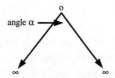

A narrow-minded, shallow person is represented by a small angle with little depth:

This is a life driven by fear, timidity, or the lust for power. Here the spiritual is consumed by narrow intent. Such a life is easily toppled and not only lives on its nerves, it gets on everybody else's nerves, too! The lust for power, for example, narrows one's focus—through ambition and self-aggrandisement—to the finite domain of material success and the acclaim or envy of the world. The person with a desire for power always makes people's lives a misery, for such desire is inevitably accompanied by the need to control the Other. This need is present, too, in religion. And here is the greatest tragedy. Those who should embrace the widest possible view of life often limit themselves to the narrowest confines of dogma, prejudice and judgement.

Someone with considerable stability and breadth of character—confident, generous, unassuming, a person of integrity who can be called upon in times of crisis— would be represented by a wide angle. A wise, profound person with a reservoir of spiritual attributes and depth of character is represented by an extension of the line o→∞ .

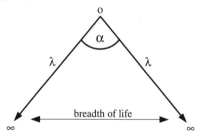

**spiritual energy is proportional to
α multiplied by λ.**

that is, se ∝ α x λ

233

What are the factors that contribute to a broad and deep state of being? One, certainly, is to develop the capacity to let go—of situations we cannot or perhaps should not control, of our ego-gravity, of the past. The genius of the Hebrew Scriptures also provides a clue. We recall the words in Genesis *Let there be...* To let things be can be risky, of course, and will always demand wisdom and discernment. Ultimately it is a question of trust in higher things.

Here then is the key to true happiness.

> **The deeper and broader one's life the less susceptible one is to the vagaries and chances of existence itself.**

Broad and deeply liberal people have a secure foundation because they are open to Life∞ and Power∞. Such people survive the storm. They are generous towards others and are rich in contentment. We know who they are. It is a joy to be in their company.

Chapter 70

A Spiritual Community

Let us therefore understand our limitations.

Blaise Pascal, *Pensées*

H umans of all religions and none relate to each other within each of the three planes of being:

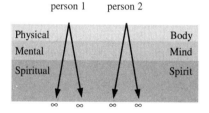

The narrower lives are the more distant, or separated, they are from each other. This can be expressed as a law:

$$S \propto \frac{p_1 \times p_2}{d^2}$$

where S is the force of spiritual attraction, p_1 and p_2 represent the spiritual quality of persons 1 and 2 respectively, and d the spiritual distance between them.

This, of course, is a parody of a law in physics! But it is obvious that any interaction between narrow lives is achieved only by drawing closer together in terms of space-time, that is, in the physical plane of being. This explains why violence, sensual pleasure, sexual activity and mob rule are often the only ways in which some people can relate to one another. If life is lived purely on the physical plane of being, with a small angle of outlook, communion with others is difficult if not impossible.

The human proclivity to material excess is entirely configurable in these simple logical terms. We may be said to have narrowed the focus of our souls to the material plane where the obvious is repeatedly emphasised, where the simple case is overstated, where noise, clamour and greed become the desired order for human life, where the ego is dependent upon artificial stimuli and feeds off simulated pleasure or anxiety. Our lives point inwards or go round the perimeter of the reduced circle of being. In effect we are cut off from the Other. This represents a loss of integrity.

> For what is a man profited, if he shall gain the
> whole world, and lose his own soul?
>
> *The Holy Bible*, Matthew 16: 26

These words are not an expression of the attitude of judgement. We are responsible for our own souls. The gain or loss is ours. But the effect is universal.

The true spiritual life is one of dynamism and creativity in the I–Other relation.

Those who have discerned the true meaning of Life$^{\infty}$ and Power$^{\infty}$, who have discovered the significance of hamartia, metanoia and aphesis for themselves and for life in general, may be said to be living in a broad and deep fellowship. In this kind of fellowship the I and the Other interact at a much more profound level.

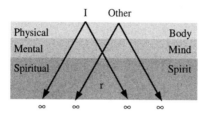

The area of interaction at 'r' indicates a kind of relationship which is lacking in the narrow-based material life.

This state of being is characterised by the ideal of true friendship. True friends are those who stick close by when the going is tough, when you are not producing the goods, or flattering your way through. A true friend is one who is prepared to share your downturn of circumstance, who sustains you by bringing hope and courage to bear through patience and fortitude. Such friendship simply cannot be institutionalised. Indeed, it can only exist in a genuine state of free will.

Chapter 71

Spiritual Love

*There is no better proof of human vanity than to
contemplate the causes and effects of love: for the
whole universe is changed by it.*

Pascal, *Pensées*

Love bade me welcome

George Herbert, *Love*

The relation I–Other is the context for the theory
and practice of what we call morality. But here
morality has nothing to do with codified
behaviour patterns that exclude by pre-judgement. It is
to do with compassion, honour, justice, freedom. In
other words, the I–Other relation needs to be
characterised by the most precious gift of all—the
virtue and fruit of love. Only here do we find the
ultimate proof and indeed test of religion.

**We experience pure religion when we invest
the I–Other relation with the right balance
between Life, Power and Love.**

In addition to the various synonyms of the Old
Testament which we have now discussed, and the
translations of what could be called the tenets of the

238

Gospel, we are presented in the New Testament with a further description of what we may understand by pure religion.

In all religions, love is the key to morality. But just as the terms of science need clear definition, so too do the objects and values of religion. The New Testament of Christian literature defines 'love' to the highest degree:

> Love is patient and kind; love is not jealous or boastful; it is not arrogant or rude. Love does not insist on its own way; it is not irritable or resentful; it does not rejoice at wrong, but rejoices in the right. Love bears all things, believes all things, hopes all things, endures all things. Love never ends.

> *The Holy Bible (RSV)*, 1 Corinthians 13: 4-8

In both Old and New Testaments we are exhorted to love the LORD GOD with all our heart, with all our soul, with all our mind and with all our strength. We are also to love our neighbour as ourselves. Ultimately we are told in Scripture that *GOD is love* (1 John 4: 8). There is a thrill in discovering a new interpretation of the commandments (Mark 12: 30):

Love *Life*$^\infty$ with all your heart, with all your soul, with all your mind and with all your strength.

Morality is the human response to the absolutes of Life$^\infty$, Power$^\infty$ and Love$^\infty$. It is the alignment of the will along the axes between them. This perhaps needs some explanation.

We all have life. We also have power in some form or other—at a level of molecular biological make-up, in

239

our minds and in our relations with the world around us. At times we have love. These are characteristics of the human being. They are also attributes of the universe.

The Trinity of Pure Religion

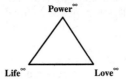

Only one pair of co-ordinate terms in the Trinity of Pure Religion contains the dynamics of perfect symmetry: Life and Love.

To have a life of love and a deep love of life is the essence of pure religion.

Life ↔ Love

The other terms are asymmetrically related and when arranged in a certain way may be said to be indicative of what is meant by aiming in the wrong direction: Love → Power; Life → Power. This is what separates the secular world from pure religion, and the world of the pseudo-liberal and the fundamentalist from the true Faith.

The pure religious life does not espouse or advocate a love of power but the power of love. It aims not at a life of power but the power of life.

The power of Life and the power of Love may be called the Fruit of the Spirit. If anyone practises the life of Love they may be said to be living in the power of the Spirit.

240

Part Thirteen

Christianity Revisited

Part Thirteen

Christianity Revisited

Chapter 72

Christ

The unsearchable riches of Christ.

The Holy Bible, Ephesians 3: 8

The question now is: what is the way ahead? In particular, Christians who have survived the book so far must be asking if we have we abandoned all that is most precious to the Christian soul simply to accommodate science and other religions in some sort of general belief. Jesus, the Cross, the Resurrection, the Church—are these to be forsaken for the sake of a universal theology? The answer is no, these have not been forsaken or surrendered. But it has been shown that they do require explanation, even exploration, before they can be considered by a rational mind and elevated into objects of faith.

There is no doubt that the person of Jesus Christ is central to the faith of Christians. He is described in the Christian Scriptures as 'the way, the truth, and the life' (John 14: 6). But the belief that Christ is the Son of GOD is a stumbling block to other Faiths and to those of no faith at all. This may or may not worry Christians but it certainly impedes unity between religions. How is this impasse to be resolved?

Christians start by giving an *historical* account of Christ. This is what I call the human interpretation and is familiar to anyone who goes to Church.

The title 'Christ', from the Greek word χριστος (Christos), means 'Messiah', 'the anointed one'. The Messiah was associated from early Hebrew times with kingship and became identified with a person whose birth was first anticipated in the Hebrew Scriptures approximately six centuries before Jesus was born. He would deliver the Israelites from servitude and into the rule of Yahweh.

Christians believe that Jesus Christ was that person. But they also believe something more. Christ, they believe, is Saviour not only of Israel but of the whole world. He delivered people from their sins and brought salvation to the human soul. Thus Christians hold that Jesus Christ was the fulfilment of prophecy, whereas the Jews do not. Christians believe that Jesus Christ was the Son of God; the Islam faith considers this to be blasphemy. Buddhists and Hindus make allowances but in the end go their own way. It seems nobody can win. Religions are determined to disagree. So perhaps we ought to leave them to it.

Or should we invite them and the modern, scientific mind to consider all possibilities? Isn't it time for Christians to reassess the meaning behind the historical Christ, to leave their prejudices and predilections on the shores of mediocrity and launch into the depths of true faith and spirituality?

Chapter 73

Universal Christianity

Men of sense are really but of one religion.

Anthony Ashley Cooper, 1st Earl of Shaftesbury

The moment has come for Christianity to rediscover its own soul with courage and conviction. It can no longer hide under the garments of false humility, afraid of reality, seeking simply to be pleasant, timorous in proclaiming the truth. Christianity is for all people or for none. It is universal, or in the original sense of the word, catholic—from κατα ὅλος (kata holos) = in respect of wholeness.

Christ is described in the New Testament Scriptures as the Word Incarnate. The Word is the creative principle of the universe.

> All things were made by him; and without him was not any thing made that was made.
>
> *The Holy Bible*, John 1: 3

Such a claim cannot be ignored. Since the Word = the Logos and the Logos is the rational principle that sustains the universe then this must mean that everything within the universe comes into being through and for a reason. St John continues:

> And the Word was made flesh, and dwelt
> among us.
>
> *The Holy Bible*, John 1: 14

That is a quite staggering claim to make. It suggests that Jesus Christ was somehow the embodiment of the rational principle of meaning and truth that exists throughout and beyond the universe, by which everything comes into being. The stars, the vast distances of space, galaxies, atoms, quarks, the laws of mathematics and physics, the enigma of time—all these are related to Christ. And this is echoed elsewhere in the New Testament.

> ...there is one God, the Father, from whom are all
> things and for whom we exist, and one Lord, Jesus
> Christ, through whom are all things and through
> whom we exist.
>
> *The Holy Bible (RSV)*, 1 Corinthians 8: 6

If we remember the two definitions:

GOD, the Father = Life$^\infty$, Power$^\infty$ and Love$^\infty$
The Lord Jesus Christ = The Logos Incarnate

then the ascription in 1 Corinthians can be understood as the foundation of the rational principle of life and the basis of a *universal pure religion,* for clearly this text refers to a metaphysical level in reality and not solely to the plane of human existence. It represents the highest level of human understanding, to which all of us can aspire.

Such texts have far reaching implications. First, they embrace the whole of humankind and not just a part of

246

it. Secondly, they dissolve the boundaries between the Church, religions, science and humankind—for these are not texts to which the Church owns the sole rights. They are texts such that anyone who believes them becomes a member of the true Faith. There is a difference. And this difference extends right across the board in religious truth.

Thus priesthood is no longer a question of defining a priest as a professional who brings others to a knowledge of eternal life, but if *anyone* brings someone to this knowledge, that person is a priest. Perhaps this is what is meant by the term 'priesthood of all believers' or, in St Paul's words:

> Ye are a chosen generation, a royal priesthood, an holy nation.
>
> *The Holy Bible,* 1 Peter 2: 9

So it is with many texts that are considered to be limited to Christians alone. Time and again we find that they are texts, rather, for the whole world. For example, Christ's words 'no one comes to the Father, but by me' (John 14:6, RSV) can, of course, be accepted in terms of the familiar language of the New Testament. But they stand quite alone, dignified and serene in their metaphysical setting.

> **No-one can come to Life$^\infty$, Power$^\infty$ and Love$^\infty$ except through the Logos. That is, if anyone *does* come to Life$^\infty$, Power$^\infty$ and Love$^\infty$ they do so through the Logos.**

We can now understand how early Christians considered Christ to be the Saviour of the world. Here is the answer to that perennial question *What about*

247

those who have never heard of Christ? Are they lost forever? No, they are not—if they live according to the principle of unity between Life, Power and Love.

This principle actually underlies the Cross. Here the Chief Priests, the political leaders and the mob sought their own life of power and followed the familiar tendency of humankind towards totalitarianism—*if you can't conquer the ideas, destroy the person behind them.* It was political correctness that put Christ on the Cross. The love of power over Christ, however, was soon inverted. The Resurrection displayed the power of life and love. Through the Cross we are all redeemed.

If we are courageous enough to question the Church's exclusive rights to the Logos it becomes possible for the pre-existent form of the earthly Christ to be identified with the rational principle of pure religion and no longer solely with a particular, historical, religion. There is then no reason why pure religion should not accept that the rational foundation of the whole universe, with its laws, its DNA, its energy, was somehow perfectly focused in the person of Jesus Christ—in his wisdom, his knowledge, his mind and his actions. There is also every reason for science to accept that Christ was able to perform what we interpret as miracles simply because he understood the laws of life and existence. He was truly the first born of the new generation, a man of supreme genius who towers above all else and with whom nothing can be compared.

The exclusivity of so much that passes for uniqueness to the Christian Faith is thus broadened to become a universal truth for all humankind. If the Church is truly to follow Christ it must surrender its title deeds to the Logos and lose itself in order to live.

Chapter 74

The Holy Spirit

*The Spirit searcheth all things, yea, the deep
things of God.*

The Holy Bible, 1 Corinthians 2: 10

The edifice of the present Church bears little
resemblance to the simple origins of
Christianity. In the New Testament there was
no institutional Church as we understand it today.
What could be called the Church, the εκκλησια
(ekklesia), was founded as a fellowship of faithful
people bound together by a common cause. The term
'ekklesia' was a common enough word in ancient
Greece. It simply meant 'gathering' or 'assembly' such
as a political meeting or a crowd of spectators. The
word 'ecclesiastical' is entirely secular in origin.

The early Christians were, however, distinguished by
the quality of their lives. Throughout the Epistles of the
New Testament they were known as saints, from the
Greek αγιοι (hagioi) meaning holy, pure, sacred,
set apart to achieve something. This described
their character as well as their beliefs. Clearly, though,
the saints were deeply practical. They cared for
one another and supported each other in a simple
and enduring way. They also lived as a spiritual

community. Their beliefs were metaphysical and not restricted to the world of space-time. They transcended the worldly domain. Even the most ordinary people had a spiritual belief that reached out to Life$^\infty$.

The spiritual relationship amongst the saints was the fellowship of το πνευμα το αγιον (to pneuma to hagion), the Holy Spirit.

The Physical World

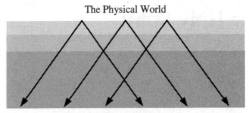

The Spiritual Dimension

The saints existed in the *power* of the Holy Spirit. In the New Testament the presence of the Holy Spirit is associated with a rushing mighty wind and with flames of fire. This poetic description of the flame perfectly captures the idea of movement, dynamism, in contrast with the idea of the crystal which represents the permanence and perfection of form in the logos. The early Christians were concerned with the content and meaning of their lives and beliefs rather than with the form of their organisation.

The Fellowship of the Holy Spirit is something in which everyone can partake. But this means much more than going to a church service or belonging to a religious institution. The Holy Spirit is present in those who have changed direction, who now point their lives towards the Infinite and are filled with the fullness of Being. By aligning themselves with the purpose of life in this way everyone can experience salvation.

250

Chapter 75

The Christian Trinity

All good things go in threes.

Proverb

The ekklesia (assembly) of the saints discovered Truth, intellectually and spiritually, by directing their lives towards heaven. Christ spoke at length about the nature of heaven. He used stories and parables to explain what otherwise would remain a baffling mystery. This was his genius. His use of analogy is unparalleled. He spoke with complete authority about metaphysical reality.

> In my Father's house are many mansions:
> if it were not so, I would have told you.

The Holy Bible, John 14: 2

We can now retranslate these words into our new language:

In the infinite reaches of Life$^\infty$, Power$^\infty$ and Love$^\infty$ there are many dimensions.

Whichever translation we prefer it is clear that Christianity was never intended to be yet another

251

religion—in competition, so to speak, with other
religions and even within itself! Life, power, love,
reason are not partisan; they do not belong to
a particular creed. They are universal and thus embrace
the whole universe of human thought, experience and
being.

Christians of course receive their understanding of
GOD from the personal formula of what is known as the
Holy Trinity—Father, Son and Holy Spirit. For them
this is the Ultimate Truth. In this book we have
discovered two further Trinities—the Trinity of Pure
Religion: power, love and life; and the Trinity of the
Person: body, mind and spirit—making a Trinity of
Trinities. Let us call this the Trinity of Being. Since
the Trinity of Being applies to reality, to the universe of
space-time and to the human frame, this extension of
the Christian Faith embraces the metaphysical, the
cosmological and the existential. The Christian Faith is
an analogy of life itself.

It is crucial to religious unity that we incorporate the
insights of all major religions into the Trinity of Being.
They have their place in the scheme of things. But it is
also important to truth that religions begin to allow for
the universality of the texts of the Jewish and Christian
faiths now they have become independent of their
institutional regulators.

Chapter 76

Prayer

He prayeth best who loveth best
All things both great and small.

S T Coleridge, *Rime of the Ancient Mariner*

Many people ask me about prayer. What is prayer? How do you pray? I can only answer by drawing attention in the first place to what I consider prayer *not* to be:

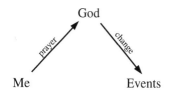

O God, help me to...
O God, I pray for x,y,z that they may...

that is, me asking God to do something in the world, to influence events, to alter things.

When people find that their prayers go unanswered this is very likely because they are identifying prayer solely with making requests. And that is sometimes the fault of organised religion.

The prayers of institutional religion are frequently 'earthed' by being too repetitive and too particular. They do not seem to take into account the grandeur and vastness of the universe with all its remarkable variations and possibilities. If ever there was a dynamic for prayer it is in this simple formula:

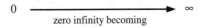

$$0 \quad \longrightarrow \quad \infty$$

zero infinity becoming

We could say that true prayer is the soul *searching* for GOD. How different that is from the familiar pattern of prayer in churches in which both the existence and nature of God are assumed, taken for granted almost, and where this God is always asked to do things, often on our behalf, in the world. Prayer is more than that.

Prayer is communion with the Infinite. It is found in the stillness of the soul and results in the quiet assurance of being, whatever the turmoil surrounding one's life.

Prayer first of all requires a *transcendent* vision of GOD as Life∞, Power∞ and Love∞. GOD can deal with things that we cannot even begin to comprehend:

> It is the imperfection of our finite nature, that we cannot at once attend to divers things, but the more vehement our intention is upon one, the greater is our neglect of the rest. But God's Infinity cannot be so bounded; his Eyes at once see, and his Providence at once orders all the most distant and disparate things in the World... he watches over us as a guardian, not as a spy.
>
> Allestree, *The Art of Contentment*

In the Lord's Prayer (Matthew 6: 9-13) we find the pattern for all prayer. Below, the transliteration from the Greek text is on the left, and our new interpretation on the right.

The first thing for us to do is to try to define, locate and meditate upon the reality of GOD:

Father of us all	**Father of all humankind**
the one in the heavens	**the unity in infinity**

After locating the true GOD in metaphysical space Christ continues with three conditions before prayer can become petitionary, that is before we can ask GOD *for* something. These are all in the imperative passive. Thus:

may your name be hallowed	**may Life[∞] be revered**
may your kingdom come	**may the order of divine unity be realised**
may your will be done	**may the order of divine law prevail**
as in heaven	**as in the infinite domain**
also on earth	**so in the finite domain of space-time.**

Only then do we find 'Give us this day our daily bread'. Even so, when Christ said that whatever we ask for it will be given (John 14:13) he supplied the condition 'in my name'—that is, in his name as 'the way, the truth and the life', the result of pointing towards the Infinite.

So in effect true prayer is the alignment of the human soul with the rational principle of the Trinity of Being. Such alignment is the metaphysical object of these petitionary words of prayer by St Paul:

255

For this reason I bow my knees before *the Father*,
from whom every family in heaven and on earth is
named,

that according to the riches of his glory he may
grant you to be strengthened with might through
his *Spirit* in the inner man,

and that *Christ* may dwell in your hearts through
faith;

that you, being rooted and grounded in love, may
have power to comprehend with all the saints
what is the breadth and length and height and
depth, and to know the love of Christ which
surpasses knowledge,

that you may be filled with all the fullness of God.

The Holy Bible (RSV), Ephesians 3: 14-19

Such prayer is not for Christians alone, it is not even
for 'religious' people. It is in fact a universal prayer—
inclusive, not exclusive, benevolent, rich and deep in its
aspirations for humankind.

Prayer is to search for the power of life and the
power of love within the eternal depths and mysteries of
the universe. It is to discover the 'unsearchable riches
of Christ' (Ephesians 3: 8) in the depths of our own souls.

The whole journey from zero to the Infinity of Being
is one of prayer. 'Laborare est orare' is a truth. But it
is also true to say 'orare est laborare'—to pray is to
work. It is within the true state of prayer that great
things begin to happen, whether we ask for them or not.

Part Fourteen

Unity

Chapter 77

The Vision of Oneness

One out of many.

Pliny the Younger

Perhaps we have now found the basis of unity between religions and between religion and science—by tracing our beliefs back to their source. That source coincides with the rise of rationality and consciousness in humankind nearly three thousand years ago.

The brilliant idea of the logos, the rational principle of the universe, was first published by Heraclitus six centuries before Christ—around the time that Siddhartha Gotama, the enlightened one, was teaching that consciousness is a mode of ultimate reality. These and the writings of the Hebrew Old Testament, which appeared during the same period, established that consciousness and rationality are not only characteristics of the universe but enable humankind to communicate with reality.

Around this time human beings were also becoming aware of the contrast between the changing and the permanent in our midst and it was this contrast more than anything else that gave rise to the great religions.

For example:

> Everything is changing. It arises and passes away.
>
> *The Dhammapada,* 20 The Path v.277

> Even as the gatherer of flowers discovers the finest and the rarest, so will you gather the teachings and transcend this world.
>
> *The Dhammapada*, 4 Flowers v.45

> The grass withereth, the flower fadeth: but the word of our God shall stand forever.
>
> *The Holy Bible*, Isaiah 40: 8

Many thinkers of the ancient world, both in the East and in the West, accepted change as the stuff of life yet searched for some factor that bound everything together—a principle of unity. For instance, in the Fragments of Heraclitus we find:

> Out of all things there is a unity, and out of unity every thing comes.
>
> Heraclitus, Fragment 25

> It is not from me but from the logos that you have heard—it is wise to agree that all things are one.
>
> Heraclitus, Fragment 26

And in the Hindu Scriptures:

> Unmoving – One – swifter than thought.
>
> *Iśā Upanishad,* §4

In parallel the writers of the Hebrew law wrote about the oneness of GOD:

Hear, O Israel: The LORD our God (יהוה,
Yahweh) is one LORD.

The Holy Bible, Deuteronomy 6: 4

It is clear that during the same period of history and in different parts of the world human minds were reaching the conclusion that there is a unity of meaning, purpose and truth behind all things, binding things together, and that it is possible for human consciousness to understand this principle and live by it. But this is not all. They began to believe that this truth could be grasped by the soul and made part of one's own being, so much so that one who existed in this condition was saved from the changes and chances of mortal life. This was the essence of religion and became known as the 'salvation of the soul'.

Chapter 78

Salvation without Prejudice

Love makes all equal.

Proverb

Ultimately the *raison d' être* of all religion could be said to be the salvation of the soul. We all want to be saved—especially from the loss of being.

Salvation represents the release of the human soul from the implications and directive power of a contingent, ever changing world.

Such release is expressed in the moderation of our character, in a lasting sense of peace, tranquillity, temperance and serenity of being. In the state of salvation the finite is absorbed into the Infinite, the human into the Divine, the mortal into the Immortal.

Our entry into Eternal Life, however, cannot depend upon a particular geographical location, the belief system of one's parents or—if moral spirituality is extended this far—on the whim of a particular god. When it comes to the truths of Life, and understanding one's soul in the light of eternity, it doesn't really matter whether you are a Christian, a Muslim, a Hindu or a Jew. If it did then the rational principle of the whole universe would break down and Truth would be forever subordinated to each individual set of circumstances, namely in this case the religion into which you were born or the set of beliefs to which you subscribe. That in itself would be irrational and incommensurate with Divine Law.

Pure religion gets rid of all these boundaries, necessary as they might have been perhaps for the development of the human soul at a certain stage in history. The situation is now quite different. We stand at the threshold of a new era. The old religions have served their purpose and will continue to serve their purpose no doubt, but—as with the process of selection in the natural order—they will either change, radically, or fade away like many of the religions of the ancient world.

Chapter 79

The Purpose of Existence

*Yet I doubt not through the ages one increasing
purpose runs,
And the thoughts of men are widened with the
process of the suns.*

Alfred, Lord Tennyson, *Locksley Hall*

The dawn of the scientific age could be said to
have taken place three or more thousand years
ago when human beings first sought to understand the nature of the universe and our place within it.

Whilst mortality and change were recognised as fact
we began to search for something beyond our mortality.
We embarked upon a journey towards the Eternal. So
could the purpose of human life and the destiny of the
universe be connected?

Nowadays, the consensus amongst scientists is that
the universe has been evolving over billions of years. It
is also reasonable to infer that it has been developing in
a certain direction—from an elementary state of the
primordial physical microcosm of bacterial life into
a state which now includes human consciousness. If
this is right, though, where is it going from here?

I believe that the ideals of pure religion—aiming
from the physical to the spiritual, from finite to
Infinite—actually coincide with the natural process of

264

evolution, where the final stage is not space-time but eternity.

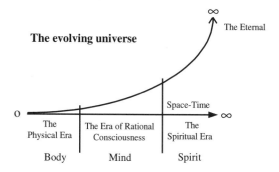

The great religious teachers have always taught that the richest and deepest life is to look towards the infinite horizon and focus on the spiritual aspect of Being. To point the other way—towards the zero of being—is not only a personal avoidance of the call of Life but also goes against the natural evolutionary direction of the universe.

Salvation is to go *with* the flow of the universe. It is to reach out towards its ultimate destination. Could this be what is meant in the New Testament by the 'kingdom of GOD'? Christ suggested that to search for the kingdom of GOD is to discover the purpose of life:

> Seek ye first the kingdom of God [Life$^\infty$]...and all these things shall be added unto you.
>
> *The Holy Bible*, Matthew 6: 33

Pure religion also teaches that each human soul can attain the goal of evolution now, in this lifetime—by

265

forsaking the priorities that characterise worldliness and releasing oneself from the gravitational attraction of mortality. Christ also said:

> The kingdom of God is within you.
>
> *The Holy Bible*, Luke 17: 21

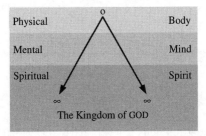

The Kingdom of GOD has its own laws of which the laws of science are an analogy. Here, in the relation between the individual and the universe, the traditional path to wisdom and the insights of science coincide.

266

Chapter 80

Letting Go

The absurd person is one who never changes.

Barthélemy

The dynamic of hope offered by pure religion in this singularly time-driven existence unites all human beings who wish to extend the scope of being beyond the finitude of their mortal lot.

Those who have embarked upon the journey of discovery and who wish to launch into the deep, in the spirit of religious explorers who have been unafraid to take risks in their intellectual and spiritual search for truth, have something in common—something very precious which needs to be cherished and nurtured. Fellowship and learning will bring such people together.

We do not speak here of further churches and temples, congregations and assemblies. For the only true temple of the spirit is Being itself. Each religion is quite free to enter the fellowship of the Divine Order of Being.

The purpose of pure religion is to encourage and inspire human beings to discover and share abundant life.

Pure religion is for all humanity. If a soul trusts itself to Divine Law and searches for the eternal within and beyond the temporal, that soul is following the path of pure religion. This change of direction from inwardness to the infinite domain of Life, Power and Love may be said to be the purpose of Life for each of us. Here, every person will discover who they are and why they exist in this universe.

Were individual religions to agree with the ideals of pure religion they would reduce their institutional trappings to the point where human beings felt free to try the spiritual journey towards the Infinite for themselves, without injunction or rule. The politics of religions would then quickly evaporate. Instead their duty and privilege would be to assist individual souls in their personal pilgrimage towards truth—through beautiful architecture, uplifting music, serene liturgies, space for prayer, interior silence and external peace, strength in solitude and by turning the mind to the deeper plane of existence through belief in the Divine Order.

The human spirit and the truths of the universe do not fade. In so far as the truths of pure religion coincide with those of reality, these truths will remain and be strengthened by their verification in human hearts and minds to lead humanity into the age of peace and goodwill. The message to all religions is to let go, to break down the barriers between them and begin to learn how to explore together the potential of life.

Epilogue

Redefining the Church

The Church exists for those outside it.

William Temple, 98th Archbishop of Canterbury

We began this little book by thinking about the Church of England, and its setting within Christianity and the world's great religions. The undoubtable facts about the decline of Christianity in the West are matched by its growth in other parts of the world, not least in the continent of Africa where there is a natural vibrancy of faith that must be the envy of the stolid European.

The Church of England itself is part of the world-wide Anglican Communion and therefore cannot be considered entirely in isolation. But we would be doing the truth, and the implications that arise from an honest recognition of the truth, serious injustice if we failed, or refused, to recognise the state of affairs that prevails at home in the National Church and its implications for developed religion.

We have seen how the Church of England is over-organised to do its job and, sadly, how it has, to a considerable extent, failed in its task to convert England. This is a solemn and sober charge. Upbeat messages from the directors of the company have left everything as before. They are bound to, if for no other reason than the fact that the theology they have held for many years is obsolete. It belongs to an era that has passed away.

In our inspection of texts and the discovery of possibilities in their translation for a new age, however, we have found a fresh hope. GOD, human life, sin, repentance and forgiveness have yielded to deeper forms of interpretation which are found to coincide with their original meanings and which speak to modern life in a way that previous translations now simply fail to do.

If by Divine grace Christianity, and the Church of England in particular, is once again to address the human condition and prepare the way for the future, then we have to begin to let go of our prejudices and our unjustifiable assumptions about the nature of the universe and start to rebuild the Faith for the centuries ahead.

But this time we have to mean it. It is after all the Christian Church that has lost sight of the rational principles that stand behind and within the universe, chiefly because we have rejected the metaphysical foundations of the Faith. And the Church thereby has lost numerous opportunities in the scientific field. It is we who have made the human, historical, Jesus the sole object of our faith and worship—precious as he is in the souls of believers—and thereby excluded the generosity of spirit that is required to search beyond Jesus for that background to our lives to which he pointed and which is so much needed in the world today, especially between religions. And it is we who have all but lost the link between the finite and the Infinite, the secular and the sacred, and thus forfeited a true understanding

270

of the nature of the universe to a secular world. The agenda of the Church now is thoroughly materialistic, with an undue emphasis on the practical and the visible. We have allowed ourselves to become too particularised and placidly domestic.

In spite of all these reservations, I believe the Christian Church is being called from the depths of creation to recreate a Faith that will embrace all religions and indeed transcend them. And I have no fear about this calling—simply because the essentials of that Faith are contained within our own inherited Holy Scriptures as a sort of hidden agenda. Outwardly this Faith will be based upon the evolutionary progress of the universe, and not stand against it; inwardly it will be built upon the foundation of the Universal Trinity of Being: Life$^\infty$, Power$^\infty$ and Love$^\infty$. Outwardly an expression of unity between the religions of the world, inwardly it will indicate the human Trinity of Body, Mind and Spirit. The aim is the restoration of integrity. That, I believe, is the purpose of the Church today.

Of course, this will incorporate the Church's traditional privileges and duties of pastoral care. But it will also necessitate a revision of some of our most cherished beliefs, and a re-ordering of the structures of the spiritual life, if we are to partake in the new order exemplified by the crystal and the flame. And perhaps a form of leadership, of the order of Abraham or Moses, will emerge from beyond the boundaries of present religion to lead us into a new world of spiritual truth.

But the main purpose, the ineffably Divine calling, will be to point the way ahead for all major religions to find that transcendent vision which will unite faiths all

271

over the world in a common belief—the belief that there is a Divine Order behind and within creation; that each person has a soul and that this soul is intended, from within the very depths of Being, to last forever in the Divine splendour from whom are all things and for whom we exist.

Psalm

You are quietness and peace,
Soul of the Universe.
You are the mystery of creation,
the unknown Spirit of life.
You are hidden in the intricacies of matter,
beyond the edge of time.

You are silence and strength,
Soul of the Universe.
You exist forever, boundless and free;
you are infinite and without frame.
Eternal Spirit of the deeps,
why do we give you a name?

You are life and existence,
Soul of the Universe.
You are the wind that moves the trees;
you are the energy of the sun.
You are the power of the mighty seas,
the endless search of man.

BIBLIOGRAPHICAL REFERENCES

Page

15   Dante Alighieri (1265-1321), *The Divine Comedy,* Inferno,
     Canto 1

21   Horace (Quintus Horatius Flaccus) (65-8 BC), *Epistles*
     1,ii.27

22   John Robinson, *The New Reformation?* SCM Press,
     London, 1965, p.101

24   Horace (Quintus Horatius Flaccus) (65-8 BC), *De arte
     poetica,* 25

24   Tobias (George) Smollett (1721-71), *The History of England
     from the Revolution to the Death of George the Second,*
     London, 1807, Vol.II

24   Jonathan Swift (1667-1745), Clergyman and satirist.
     Dean of St. Patrick's from 1714. Cited in C H Sisson,
     Is There a Church of England? Carcanet Press Limited,
     Manchester, 1993, p.241

25   C H Sisson, *Is There a Church of England? Reflections
     on Permanence and Progression,* Carcanet Press Limited,
     Manchester, 1993, p.241

26   Dick Clement & Ian La Frenais, *Whatever Happened to the
     Likely Lads?* Reproduced by permission.

26   Dr David Voas, Department of Sociological Studies,
     University of Sheffield, 'Is Britain a Christian Country?'
     2002

29   Jean-Paul Sartre, *Notebooks for an Ethics,* translated by
     David Pellauer, The University of Chicago, 1992, p.3.
     Copyright © 1992 by The University of Chicago

41   William H Seward (1801-72), American politician; Speech,
     11 March 1850.

44   *Church Representation Rules,* Church House Publishing,
     London, 1995, p.35, §36(5). Extract from *Church
     Representation Rules* is copyright © The Central Board of
     Finance of the Church of England 1984, 1990, 1992, 1995,
     1996; The Archbishops' Council 1999, 2001 and is
     reproduced by permission.

Page

47   Kenneth M. Macmorran, *Cripps on Church and Clergy*,
8th ed., Sweet and Maxwell Limited, London, 1937, p.288.

53   Sir William Jones (1746-94), English jurist, *Ode in Imitation of Alcaeus*

53   *The Encyclopaedic Dictionary* Vol.III, Cassell & Company,
London, 1887

56   Percy Bysshe Shelley (1792-1822), *Prometheus Unbound*,
Act I.

56   St Augustine of Hippo, (354-430), *De Baptismo contra Donatistas,* Bk.4, ch.17, sect.24

56   St Cyprian, (c.200-258), *Epistle Ad Pomponium, De Virginibus*, sect.4

58   James T Cushing, *Philosophical Concepts in Physics*,
Cambridge University Press, 1998, p.173

65   Jonathan Swift (1667-1745), *Thoughts on Various Subjects*

68   Thomas Carlyle (1795-1881), *Burns*

70   Johann Wolfgang von Goethe (1749-1832), German poet,
novelist and dramatist

76   Napoleon I (1769-1821), Emperor of France 1804-15

77   Adonis (Ali Ahmed Said), *An Introduction to Arab Poetics*,
translated from the Arabic by Catherine Cobham, Saqi
Books, London, 1990, p.99. Copyright © Saqi Books

77   Peter Demianovich Ouspensky (1878-1947), *A New Model of the Universe*, 2nd ed., 1934, preface.

79   Augustine Birrell, (1850-1933), British Essayist, *Obiter Dicta*, 'Carlyle'

80   Pierre Chaunu (ed.), *The Reformation*, Alan Sutton, (Sutton
Publishing Ltd.), Gloucester, 1989, pp.286,288

85   Alfred, Lord Tennyson (1809-92), English poet, *Morte d'Arthur*

87   Horace (Quintus Horatius Flaccus) (65-8 BC), *Epode* 14

92   Don Cupitt, *The Revelation of Being*, SCM Press Ltd.,
London, 1998, pp.62,75,89

97   Martin Luther (1483-1546), German Protestant theologian

99   David Collyer, Vicar of Great Coxwell, Berks., *The Sacred
Interpreter* or *A Practical Introduction towards a Beneficial
Reading and a Thorough Understanding of The Holy Bible*,
Vol.I, London, 1726, p.26

Page

102 George Steiner, *Language and Silence,* Faber and Faber, London, 1985, p.112

105 John Locke (1632-1704), *Essay on the Human Understanding,* Dedicatory Epistle.

106 Richard Dawkins, *Unweaving the Rainbow: Science, Delusion and the Appetite for Wonder,* Allen Lane The Penguin Press, London, 1998, pp.22-23. Copyright © Richard Dawkins 1998. Reproduced by permission of Penguin Books Ltd.

108 Letter from 'N.B' to *The Spectator,* Feb.27, 1711-12. Bound publication: *The Spectator,* Volume the Fourth, Edinburgh, 1766, p.292

109 Marion M Scott, *Beethoven,* (Master Musician Series), J M Dent and Sons Ltd, London, 1934, pp.117, 125. Reprinted by permission of Oxford University Press.

109 Ernest Newman, *The Unconscious Beethoven,* Parsons, London, 1927, cited in Marion M Scott, *Beethoven,* J M Dent and Sons Ltd, London, 1934, p.122

111 *The Spectator,* December 5, 1712. Bound publication: *The Spectator,* Volume the Seventh, Edinburgh, 1766, p.367

112 Italo Calvino, *Six Memos for the Next Millennium,* trans. Patrick Creagh, Jonathan Cape, London, 1992, p.70-71. Used by permission of the Random House Group Limited.

115 *Secret Museums: Alberto Giacometti & Tahar Ben Jelloun,* trans. Alan Sheridan, Flohic Editions, Paris, 1991

115 J.D. McClatchy (ed.), *Poets on Painters: Essays on the Art of Painting by Twentieth-Century Poets,* University of California Press, 1990

115 Jacques Maritain, *Creative Intuition in Art and Poetry: The A W Mellon Lectures in the Fine Arts,* Bollingen Series XXXV•1, Pantheon Books, New York, 1955

115 Ernst Neizvestny, *Space, Time, and Synthesis in Art: Essays on Art, Literature, and Philosophy,* ed. Albert Leong, Mosaic Press, New York, 1990.

115 Andrey Tarkovsky, *Sculpting in Time: Reflections on the Cinema,* trans. Kitty Hunter-Blair, Faber and Faber, London, 1989

Page

115 Jay Belloli (ed.), *The Universe: A Convergence of Art, Music, and Science*, Armory Center for the Arts, Pasadena, California, 2001

116 Arthur Stanley Eddington, mathematician and astronomer. Reproduced by permission.

117 Ben Nicholson (1934), cited in Maurice de Sausmarez (ed.), *Ben Nicholson*, a Studio International Special, Studio International, London & New York, 1969, p.31. Courtesy of the Studio Trust

119 Algernon Charles Swinburne (1837-1909), English poet, *Dedication,* 1865

119 Martin Buber (1878-1965), *I and Thou*, T & T Clark, 1984

120 William Wordsworth (1770-1850), English poet, *Lines Written a few miles above Tintern Abbey*

123 Samuel Johnson (1709-1784), English poet, critic and lexicographer; letter to Boswell, 1774

125 Thomas à Kempis (c.1380-1471), *Of the Imitation of Christ*, trans./ed. The Ven W H Hutchings, Longmans, Green, and Co, London, 1905, p.5

126 Pope John Paul II, *Faith and Reason*, Catholic Truth Society, London, 1998, pp.3,95

127 Sir Francis Bacon (Lord Verulam and Viscount St. Albans) (1560-1626), *Proficience and Advancement of Learning*, Bk 2.

128 G E Moore, *Some Main Problems of Philosophy*, George Allen & Unwin Ltd., (Harper Collins Publishers Ltd.) London, 1962, p.2. Copyright © 1953 G E Moore

128 Isaiah Berlin, *The Power of Ideas*, ed. Henry Hardy, Chatto & Windus, London, 2000, p.34. Reproduced with permission of Curtis Brown Group Ltd, London, on behalf of the Isaiah Berlin Literacy Trust. © Isaiah Berlin 1962

130 Bertrand Russell, 'The Free Man's Worship', *The Collected Papers of Bertrand Russell*, Volume XII, ed. R A Rempel, A Brink & M Moran, George Allen & Unwin, London, 1985, pp.66,67

133 John Rotheram, Rector of Ryton, *An Essay on Faith, and its Connection with Good Works*, London, 1768, p.230

Page

135 Lancelot Andrewes (1555-1626), Bishop of Winchester,
*A Collection of Posthumous and Orphan Lectures delivered
at St Pauls and St Giles his church*, London, 1657, p.5

137 C H Dodd, *The Fourth Gospel*, Cambridge University Press,
1953, p.263

142 Wolfhart Pannenberg, *Metaphysics and the Idea of God,*
trans. Philip Clayton, T & T Clark, Edinburgh, 1990, p.6

144 J G Zimmerman, *Solitude*, London, 1805, Vol.II, p.165

146 J G Zimmerman, *Solitude*, London, 1804, Vol.I, p.32

148 Johann Wolfgang von Goethe (1749-1832), German poet,
novelist and dramatist.

151 Werner Heisenberg, *Physics and Philosophy*, Penguin
Books, London, 1989, p.135

157 Percy Bysshe Shelley (1792-1822), *Queen Mab*, Canto 1

157 Leo Tolstoy, *A Confession and Other Religious Writings*,
trans. Jane Kentish, Penguin Classics, London, 1987, p.134.
Copyright © Jane Kentish 1987. Reproduced by permission
of Penguin Books Ltd.

159 Percy Bysshe Shelley (1792-1822), *Prometheus Unbound*,
Act 2, 4

162 Kenneth Verity, *Awareness Beyond Mind*, Element Books,
Shaftesbury, Dorset, 1996, p.5 (reprinted by Vega Books,
London, 2002)

162 Paul Tillich, *The Shaking of the Foundations*, Penguin
Books (Pelican), London, 1963, p.63. First published by
SCM Press 1949

163 William Langland (c.1332-1400), *The Vision of William
concerning Piers the Plowman*, Passus 12, l.129

165 Albert Einstein, *The Meaning of Relativity*, Chapman and
Hall, London, 1980, pp.1,2

172 David Collyer, Vicar of Great Coxwell, Berks., *The Sacred
Interpreter* or *A Practical Introduction towards a Beneficial
Reading and a Thorough Understanding of The Holy Bible*,
Vol.I, London, 1726, p.27 (footnote)

177 Robert G Ingersoll (1833-99), American agnostic, *The Gods*,
pt.1, 1876

Page

178 Bradley W Carroll & Dale A Ostlie, *An Introduction to Modern Astrophysics*, Addison-Wesley Publishing Company Inc. (USA), 1996, p.1289

179 Sir Isaac Newton (1642-1727), *Principia Mathematica* 'Scholium Generale'

180 Stephen Hawking, *A Brief History of Time*, Bantam Press, London, 1996, p.181. Extract used by permission of Transworld Publishers, a division of The Random House Group Limited.

182 Matthew Prior (1664-1721), *Solomon*, Bk.1, l.740

184 Paul Davies, *The Mind of God*, Penguin Books, London, 1993, p.58. First published by Simon & Schuster UK. Copyright © Orion Productions 1992

188 John Milton (1608-74), *Areopagitica*

197 Clemens Alexandrinus, Titus Flavius Clemens or Clement of Alexandria (AD 150-220), *Strom.* i 5, cited in Henry Melvill Gwatkin, *Selections from Early Christian Writers*, Macmillian and Co., London, 1937, p.107

198 Percy Bysshe Shelley (1792-1822), *A Defense of Poetry*, ed. Albert S Cooke, The Athenaeum Press, Boston, 1890, p.1

203 William Wordsworth (1770-1850), *The Excursion,* Bk.3

205 Thomas Moore (1779-1852), *Paradise and the Peri*

209 John Davison, B.D. Fellow of Oriel College, Oxford. *Discourses on Prophecy...being the substance of twelve sermons preached in the Chapel of Lincoln's Inn*, 1849

220 Sir Walter Scott (1771-1832), *The Lady of the Lake*, Canto 1

222 Aeschylus (c.525-456 BC), *Prometheus Bound*, line 515

229 Samuel Rogers (1763-1855), English poet, *Italy*, 'Bologna'

229 Samuel Beckett, *How It Is*, John Calder, London, 1977, p.15

235 Blaise Pascal, *Pascal's Pensées,* trans. Martin Turnell, Harvill Press, London, 1962, p.218 no. 390. Reproduced by permission of the Harvill Press.

238 Blaise Pascal, ibid., p.213 no. 388. Reproduced by permission of the Harvill Press.

238 George Herbert (1593-1632), *The Church: Love (III)*.

245 Anthony Ashley Cooper (1621-83), First Earl of Shaftesbury, cited in Bishop Gilbert Burnet, *History of My Own Time*, 1724, Vol.I, Bk.2, Ch.1

Page

253 Samuel Taylor Coleridge (1772-1834), *Rime of the Ancient Mariner*, Pt.7

254 Allestree, *The Art of Contentment*, At the Theater in Oxford, 1689, p.120

259 Pliny the Younger (Caius Caecilius Secundus (AD c.61-c.112), Roman senator and writer, Epistles, Bk.1, 3

260 Anne Bancroft (ed.), *The Dhammapada*, Element, Shaftesbury, Dorset, 1997, (Reprinted by Vega Books, London 2002)

260 Heraclitus (c.540-480 BC), Fragment 25, 26. Translated by the author from the Greek text in M Marcovich, *Heraclitus,* Los Andes University Press, Merida, Venuezela, 1967, pp.102,111.

260 Hindu Scriptures: *Iśā Upanishad*, trans./ed. R C Zaehner, Everyman's Library, 1992, p.209, §4

264 Alfred, Lord Tennyson (1809-92), *Locksley Hall*

267 Jules Barthélemy St. Hilaire (1805-1895)

269 William Temple, (1881-1944), Archbishop of Canterbury from 1942